Praise fo[illegible]

"As human beings we are ca[illegible] positive change. Google engineer Chade-Meng Tan's book, *Search Inside Yourself,* which creatively blends the ancient meditative practice of mindfulness with the contemporary field of emotional intelligence, shows that to avoid certain kinds of results, you need to change the conditions that give rise to them. If you change the habitual patterns of your mind, you can change their resulting attitudes and emotions and find peace and inner happiness."

—His Holiness the Dalai Lama

"This is a book offering much good advice. I most appreciate Meng's insight that expressing compassion for others brings happiness to oneself as well."

—Jimmy Carter, 39th president of the United States

"At a time when so many books are being published on such subjects as leadership, strategy, governance, and other topics, I applaud Chade-Meng for daring to undertake the writing of such a book on 'emotional intelligence,' within which lies the core essence of knowing oneself. The advice and practices he offers will help improve all aspects of our lives and in the process lead to a world where greater peace and happiness are possible."

—S. R. Nathan, 6th president of Singapore

"This book and the course it's based on represent one of the greatest aspects of Google's culture—that one individual with a great idea can really change the world."

—Eric Schmidt, executive chairman of Google

"Meng is like a wise and humorous monk who will continue to inspire you for years after you close the pages of his book. Written with the needs of today's world in mind, *Search Inside Yourself* offers practical and proven tools wrapped in the gift of timeless wisdom."

—John Mackey, co-chief executive officer and co-founder of Whole Foods Market

"Combining timeless wisdom with modern science, Chade-Meng Tan has created an entertaining and practical guide to success and happiness."

—Deepak Chopra

"Mahatma Gandhi said to turn the spotlight, the searchlight, inwards.

Meng has done it, showing us how to join him in following these peaceful and profound, loving and compassionate footsteps in developing the mindful-based emotional wisdom that can help us be serene and feel in harmony, and contribute to a better world. Practical, accessible, broad, and deep; with his Inner Search tools, tips, techniques—and delightful illustrations—our friend has made a truly awakening contribution to this troubled cacophonous Over-Information Age. I heartily recommend it to all those aspiring to self-mastery, attention training and focus, spiritual wisdom, and the joy-path of the wakeful life through everyday enlightened living. Seek, and ye shall find. This book is one of the very best places to start."

—Lama Surya Das

"This book reveals a key part of the secret behind the success of Google. It is a touchstone for those of us interested in revolutionizing the many outdated institutions and systems in our country. Whether we are trying to create positive change in education, health care, the corporate realm, or in our personal relationships, *Search Inside Yourself* teaches us that external positive change can only happen if we each individually spend time each day cultivating a better understanding of our own inner world."

—Tim Ryan, U.S. congressman and author of *A Mindful Nation*

"Full of humor and humility, wisdom and mindfulness, Chade-Meng Tan's book is a compelling read, but more importantly, it's a valuable operating manual for living a good life. Rarely have I read a book that's full of so much intelligence and emotion. I want to be Meng when I grow up!"

—Chip Conley, founder of Joie de Vivre Hotels and author of *Emotional Equations*

"*Search Inside Yourself* is a practical guide to the fundamentals of emotional intelligence. This book has the potential to change lives and deliver happiness."

—Tony Hsieh, *New York Times* bestselling author of *Delivering Happiness* and CEO of Zappos

"Chade-Meng Tan has a voice that modern people can readily listen to: consciousness informed with science. More than that, he has something to say of real importance for our time—that global peace depends on the personal experience that meditation leads to. Old wisdom is presented here with a provocative and startling freshness. The way to enlightenment begins with waking up. Meng is doing this with passion, humor, and generosity of mind. This is a book to read, share, laugh with, and celebrate."

—Father Laurence Freeman, OSB, director of the World Community for Christian Meditation

"There is more to be discovered inside of ourselves than we will ever find by searching anywhere else, and the challenge is in learning how to look. In a simple and plainspoken way, Meng has crafted an elegant invitation we can all use to take that journey."

—Scott Kriens, chairman of Juniper Networks and director of 1440 Foundation

"Meng inspires all with his modesty, humor, intelligence, and—dare I say it?—love. Meeting Meng, I experienced a kind of radiant vicarious love. In this book, you too can have a vicarious love affair with some of Meng's spiritual friends: wisdom, compassion, and equanimity.

Meng shows you where the tools are hidden inside of you, mapping your way with the precise logic of an engineer, encouraging you with the compassion of a longtime meditator, and in an ironic twist, seducing you to press 'pause' on the incessant drone of technology and modernity in the outside world, just long enough to find joy within you in the ancient wisdom, on the path eternal."

—Larry Brilliant, president of the Skoll Global Threats Fund

"Chade-Meng has written an excellent book that should be read by everyone. This great work restores emotional intelligence and its underlying traits, compassion, awareness, and empathy, or at least underscores the need for these attributes in our society. It is no surprise that the best venture capitalists and entrepreneurs I know all possess the attributes that Chade-Meng alludes to. In my opinion, this is one of the best works ever in personal development and a refreshing change from so much verbiage out there in other works. Read this book, and it will profoundly change your life."

—Tan Yinglan, author of *The Way of the VC* and *Chinnovation*

"I began reading his book with a somewhat patronizing attitude, like an uncle going through a nephew's writings. As I leafed through the pages, I found myself sitting up, poring over the words more carefully and reflecting on what he had to say with increasing seriousness. When I visited Qom a couple of years ago, a Grand Ayatollah gave as his parting words to me: May you find what you seek. I have long thought about what the Grand Ayatollah said. Chade-Meng's book has pointed me in the right direction."

—Brigadier-General George Yeo, former minister for foreign affairs, Singapore

SEARCH INSIDE YOURSELF

The Unexpected Path to Achieving Success, Happiness (and World Peace)

CHADE-MENG TAN

Illustrations by Colin Goh

HarperOne
An Imprint of HarperCollins*Publishers*

HarperOne

HarperCollins books may be purchased for educational, business, or sales promotional use. For information please write: Special Markets Department, HarperCollins Publishers, 10 East 53rd Street, New York, NY 10022.

HarperCollins website: http://www.harpercollins.com

FIRST EDITION

Artwork by Colin Goh. Used by permission.

Library of Congress Cataloging-in-Publication Data is available upon request.

ISBN 978–0–06–211692–5
ISBN 978–0–06–220456–1 (int'l)

13 14 15 16 RRD(H) 10 9 8 7 6 5 4 3

Once upon a time, there was a world-renowned expert in emotional intelligence who was also a very talented writer. He was encouraged by his friend to write a book on mindfulness and emotional intelligence. He felt inspired to do so but could never find the time. So the friend wrote the book instead. I am that friend, and this is the book.

Thank you, Danny,
for trusting me to write this book.

Contents

Foreword

Daniel Goleman

My first impression of Google was shaped by Chade-Meng Tan, widely known as Meng. Meng is the company's unofficial greeter, its irrepressible jolly good fellow ("which nobody can deny," as his business card puts it).

As I've gotten to know him, I have realized that Meng is someone special. One tip-off came as I went by his office and saw the bulletin board on the wall near his door: row after row of Meng in snapshots with the world's bold-face names. Meng with Al Gore. Meng with the Dalai Lama. And with Muhammad Ali and with Gwyneth Paltrow. Later I learned, via a front-page article in the *New York Times,* that Meng was famous as "that Google guy," the singular engineer with high enough social intelligence to make any visitor feel right at home—and pose for a photo with him.

But that's not what makes Meng so special. Rather, it is Meng's magical combination of brilliant systems analysis with a heart of gold.

First, the analysis.

I had come to give a talk on emotional intelligence as part of the Authors@Google lecture series. I felt a bit like yet another of the endless perks employees there famously enjoy, somewhere between a massage and all the soda you can drink.

In this bastion of the intellect—after all, you need top SAT scores just to be considered for a job at Google—I anticipated that lecture with some trepidation about anyone in this hardheaded information engineering company being much interested in hearing about soft skills. So I was amazed on arriving at the room where I was to speak, the largest venue in that part of the Googleplex, to find the place overflowing, with throngs spilling into the hall. There was clearly high interest.

At Google I was talking to perhaps the highest-IQ audience I'd ever addressed. But among all those big brains who heard me that day, it was Meng who had the smarts to reverse engineer emotional intelligence. Meng picked it apart and put it back together again with a brilliant insight: he saw that knowing yourself lies at the core of emotional intelligence, and that the best mental app for this can be found in the mind-training method called mindfulness.

That insight underlies the program Meng has developed. When he unveiled the course at Google University, it was called (fittingly for a company all about web search) Search Inside Yourself. As you'll read here, many who have taken the course at Google have found it to be a transformative experience.

Meng was also savvy in choosing his collaborators, like Zen teacher Norman Fischer, and my longtime friend and colleague Mirabai Bush, founding director of the Center for Contemplative Mind in Society. And Meng has drawn on the expertise of another old friend, Jon Kabat-Zinn, who pioneered the use of mindfulness in medical settings throughout the world. Meng knows quality. He didn't stop there. Meng and this team also cherry-picked the best from well-tested methods for creating a life with self-awareness and well-being, kindness, and happiness.

Now for that heart of gold.

When Meng saw that this inner search had such benefits, his instinct was to share it with anyone who might want to give it a try—not just those lucky enough to have access to a Google course. In fact, the very first time I met Meng, he was passionate in telling me that his life goal was to bring world peace through spreading inner peace and compassion. (Meng's enthusiasm for this goal, I noticed a bit uneasily, seemed to inspire him to a level of vociferousness.)

His vision, detailed in this highly enjoyable account, entails beta testing a mindfulness-based emotional intelligence curriculum at Google and then offering it to anyone who might benefit—as he puts it, "give it away as one of Google's gifts to the world."

As I've gotten to know Meng better, I have come to realize that he is not your average engineer; he's a closet Bodhisattva. And with this book, I'd drop the "closet" part.

—Daniel Goleman

Foreword

Jon Kabat-Zinn

When I first met Meng, I thought to myself: "Who *is* this guy, who calls himself the jolly good fellow of Google?" (It is on his business card, along with the rubric "which nobody can deny.")

Meng had invited me to give a tech talk on the subject of mindfulness at Google. Within a few seconds of my arrival, he was talking to me about mindfulness and world peace, while making one joke after another. His sense of humor was a bit bewildering. Meng proceeded to take me on a tour. The first stop was his photo board in the lobby of the main building of the Googleplex . . . photos of himself together with pretty much every famous and powerful person in the world. "Who is this guy who welcomes all these heads of state, Nobel laureates, and celebrities to Google? And can I take him seriously? Can I believe everything he is telling me?"

He was telling me a lot, including that his ultimate aim was to create the conditions for world peace in his lifetime and that he felt the way to do that was to make the benefits of meditation accessible to humanity. And that Google could play a special role, being Google.

You can imagine what was going on in my head: "Google, the quintessence of universal accessibility (except in countries that try to block or regulate access to it), is interested in playing such a role in the world!? Or at least, one visionary person at Google. Amazing. Maybe he is feigning craziness and is really the one sane person around. Because he is employee number 107, he must be very good at what he was originally hired to do; that's obvious. I doubt it was just to be a jolly good fellow while everybody else was working on writing code for the next next thing."

These were the kinds of thoughts that were going through my mind at the time of my first visit. If Meng was serious about this, beyond all the humor, the potential impact and import struck me as boundless. I was duly impressed by the graphical display he pointed out in the main lobby, which showed a rotating globe with colored lights streaming into the blackness of space from everywhere on Earth where Google searches were being conducted at that moment. The different colors represented the different languages being used, and the lengths of the lines of light were proportional to the number of searches being conducted from that part of the world. Meanwhile, the subjects of all those searches were streaming down another big screen. Together, these displays imparted a moving and very visceral sense of the interconnectedness of our world—akin to the emotional impact of seeing for the first time the image of Earth in the blackness of space, taken from the moon. They also conveyed, to use Google-speak, the power of search—and the power of Google.

I won't tell you about the talks I wound up giving at Google or about my colleagues, who Meng talks about in the book, who also gave lectures in that series. They are all on YouTube, which is part of Google. And I won't tell you about the mindfulness-based stress reduction (MBSR) classes at Google that Meng instituted there and that have been ongoing now for years. Nor will I tell you about the mindfulness-based emotional intelligence program, Search Inside Yourself, that Meng developed in parallel, with a team of remarkable people who originally came to visit because it was Google and because he was Meng. That is what this book is about.

What I would like to tell you about is what I discovered about Meng from reading this book, and what you might want to keep in mind as you make your way through it—because this is not simply a book but also a curriculum, a pathway you can follow with specific exercises and guidance, a meditative approach to relating to others and to yourself that, if you engage in it systematically, is profoundly transformative and freeing—and also hopefully fun. In fact, if you discover, after giving it a fair try, that it is not fun or doesn't at least give you a sense of being personally compelling and potentially nurturing of what is deepest and best in yourself, perhaps it is not the right moment for you to undertake the entirety of the Search Inside Yourself program. But the seeds will inexorably have been planted just by reading the book and playing around with the exercises in whatever ways make sense to you at the moment, an open-ended experiment and adventure in mental and emotional fitness and its applications in your life, and in your work and calling.

What I discovered, and you will too, is that, all kidding aside, Meng is a very serious guy, and he is absolutely committed, as you will soon see, to mindfulness, creating the conditions for world peace, and making peacefulness the default mode on this planet, at least among the human species. And he is serious about using the platform and the power of Google to make it happen. I am guessing that was his strategy from the very beginning, in inviting meditation teachers, Buddhist scholars, and scientists who were studying contemplative practices from both the clinical and neuroscientific perspectives, and their applications in the fields of medicine and health, education, and beyond to give these talks at Google. It was a way of setting the stage for his plan to tip the world in the direction of peace. First Google, then the world.

I get the sense that Meng is so serious about his vision that he knows that taking something as important as mindfulness and its potential to transform the world too seriously would not necessarily be a good thing. So he leavens it with humor that is deadly (or maybe I should say "alively") serious. Meng's sense of humor may be an acquired taste, but I think that in reading the book, you, the reader, will quickly acquire that taste, and along with it and much more importantly, a taste for what it is pointing to, a taste of your own deep interior resources for acting in your own best interest by realizing that your interest is best served by recognizing and nurturing the interests of others at the same time.

This is what mindfulness-based emotional intelligence is all about. This is why it is so important, in so many ways, to literally and metaphorically search inside yourself. What is here to be discovered, or uncovered, is the full spectrum of who you already are as a person and the realization of how embedded you are in the multidimensional warp and woof of humanity and all life. And because mindfulness is not about getting someplace else—but rather about being fully where you already are and realizing the power of your full presence and awareness right now, in this moment—Meng's program is really about finding rather than searching. It is about dis-covering, re-covering, and un-covering that full dimensionality of your being that is already yours and then developing and refining it through systematic cultivation and practice. From there, in combination with what you most love and with your imagination and innate creativity, it is bound to manifest in the world in any number of hopefully skillful ways, in the service of our mutual well-being and happiness.

If this sounds like a utopia, it isn't. But if it sounds like a practical strategy for a more peaceful world, inwardly and outwardly, individually and collectively, locally and globally—well, it is. And that is exactly how Meng intends to play it. Having developed this program at Google and road tested it in that workplace environment, he is now ready, with this book and what will follow from it, to make the program available to the world in the spirit of open sourceware.

The curriculum of Search Inside Yourself is free. It can be used in many ways, in many venues, as you will see for yourself. The limits of its usefulness or adaptability are really only the limits of your imagination and embodiment. The Search Inside Yourself curriculum rests on an ocean of meditative wisdom practices that cultivate mindfulness, loving kindness, compassion, joy, equanimity, embodied presence, emotional intelligence, and many other fundamental aspects of our minds and hearts and bodies that are also available to you once you enter through this portal. As Meng makes abundantly clear, his aim is to "make the benefits of meditation accessible to humanity" and as accepted in the mainstream as the lifelong benefits of exercise. And, even more importantly, to ensure, to whatever degree possible, that they are implemented, lived, and enacted by each of us who might be touched by this invitation to search inside ourselves.

To this end, Meng has laid out a well-designed and well-tested pathway for the development and application of emotional intelligence in the workplace and at home. It is founded on cutting-edge science and the well-established track record of research in emotions and emotional intelligence, the importance of optimism, and the power of compassion and kindness as well as the growing neuroscientific study of mindfulness and compassion. This research is showing that significant benefits of meditation can be observed after only eight weeks of training. Richie Davidson and I did a study with a number of our colleagues showing that people in a work setting who practiced mindfulness in the form of MBSR for eight weeks showed a shift in their emotional set point in the prefrontal cortex in a direction of greater emotional intelligence, and in the same direction as monks who had practiced for over ten thousand hours—evidence that you don't have to become a monastic, or quit your job, or abandon your family to benefit from meditation. In fact, work and family are perfect environments for working with your own mind and body, cognitions, and emotions in the ways Meng describes here. Before that study was done, it was generally thought that one's emotional set point was fixed before adulthood and could not be changed. Our results showed that the brain responds to this kind of meditative training by reorganizing its activity in the direction of greater emotional balance. Other studies have shown that the brain reorganizes its very structure as well, an example of the phenomenon known as neuroplasticity.

It turns out that Meng is indeed a unique and skillful, if way out-of-the-box, meditation teacher, as depicted in the tongue-in-cheek cartoons. He is the first to say that he learned it all from others. He certainly has great teachers and collaborators in the form of Dan Goleman, Mirabai Bush, Norman Fischer, and others. But Meng himself puts it all together here in a very effective way and documents his sources assiduously. If *Search Inside Yourself* is a bit light on the time recommended for the actual formal meditation practices, that is by design. Once one has tasted the practice for oneself, the motivation is very likely to be there to extend the time of formal practice, not to achieve a special state, but to simply rest in awareness itself, outside of time altogether. This is the practice of non-doing, of openhearted presencing, of pure awareness, coextensive with and inseparable from compassion. It is not an escape from life. On the contrary, the practice of mindfulness is a gateway into the experience of interconnectedness and interdependence out of which stem emotionally intelligent actions, new ways of being, and ultimately greater happiness, clarity, wisdom, and kindness—at work and in the world. One small shift in the way we each conduct ourselves, and the crystal lattice structure of the world is already different. In this way, we are the world, and when we take responsibility for our small but not insignificant part of it, the whole is already different—the flowering we manifest emotionally and in every other way of some importance, potentially enormous.

I wish you well in entering Meng's world and Meng's mind, and more importantly, in discovering your own mind and heart and body and relationships, perhaps in new and undreamed-of ways. May your adventure here be deeply nurturing. And may it bring peace—inwardly and in every other way.

—Jon Kabat-Zinn

INTRODUCTION

Searching Inside Yourself

Look within; within is the fountain of all good.

—Marcus Aurelius

What does the happiest man in the world look like? He certainly does not look like me. In fact, he looks like a bald French guy in Tibetan robes. His name is Matthieu Ricard.

Matthieu was born and grew up in France. In 1972, after completing his Ph.D. in molecular genetics at the Institut Pasteur, he decided to become a Tibetan Buddhist monk. I tell him that the reason he became a monk is because he could not join Google back in 1972—and the monk thing seemed like the next best career choice.

Matthieu's career choice leads us to the story of how Matthieu became the "happiest man in the world." When the Dalai Lama became interested in the science of meditation, he invited Tibetan Buddhist monks to participate in scientific studies. Matthieu was an obvious choice as a subject, as he was a bona fide scientist, understood both Western and Tibetan ways of thinking, and had decades of classical meditation training. Matthieu's brain became the subject of numerous scientific studies.[1]

One of many measurements conducted on Matthieu was his level of happiness. There turns out to be a way to gauge happiness in the brain: by measuring the relative activation of a certain part of your left prefrontal cortex versus your right prefrontal cortex.[2] The stronger the relative left-tilt is measured in a person, the more that person reports positive emotions, such as joy, enthusiasm, high energy, and so on. The reverse is also true; those with higher activity on the right report negative emotions. When Matthieu's brain was scanned, his happiness measure was completely off the charts. He was, by far, the happiest person ever measured by science. Pretty soon, the popular media started nicknaming him the "happiest man in the world." Matthieu himself is a little annoyed by that nickname, which creates an element of humorous irony.

Extreme happiness is not the only cool feat Matthieu's brain can pull off. He became the first person known to science able to inhibit the body's natural startle reflex—quick facial muscle spasms in response to loud, sudden noises. Like all reflexes, this one is supposed to be outside the realm of voluntary control, but Matthieu can control it in meditation. Matthieu also turns out to be an expert at detecting fleeting facial expression of emotions known as microexpressions. It is possible to train people to detect and read microexpressions, but Matthieu and one other meditator, both untrained, were measured in the lab and performed two standard deviations better than the norm, outperforming all the trained professionals.

The stories of Matthieu and other masters of contemplative practices are deeply inspiring. These masters demonstrate that each of us can develop an extraordinarily capable mind that is, first and foremost, profoundly peaceful, happy, and compassionate.

The methods for developing such an extraordinarily capable mind are accessible even to you and me. That's what this book is about.

"Monsieur Ricard? Some deer to see you about learning to inhibit their startle reflexes."

In Google, the effort to make these methods widely accessible began when we asked ourselves this question: what if people can also use contemplative practices to help them succeed in life and at work? In other words, what if contemplative practices can be made beneficial both to people's careers and to business bottom lines? Anything that is both good for people and good for business will spread widely. If we can make this work, people around the world can become more successful at achieving their goals. I believe the skills offered here will help create greater peace and happiness in your life and the lives of those around you, and that peace and happiness can ultimately spread around the world.

To promote innovation, Google generously allows its engineers to spend 20 percent of their time working on projects outside their core jobs. A group of us used our "20 percent time" to work on what became Search Inside Yourself. We ended up creating a mindfulness-based emotional intelligence curriculum with the help of a very diverse group of extremely talented people, including a Zen master, a CEO, a Stanford University scientist, and Daniel Goleman, the guy who literally wrote the book on emotional intelligence. It sounds almost like the prelude to a good joke ("A Zen master and a CEO walked into a room . . .").

"Here we follow the Tao Jones Index."

The name of the mindfulness-based emotional intelligence curriculum is Search Inside Yourself. Like many things in Google, that name started as a joke but finally stuck. I eventually became the first engineer in Google's history to leave the engineering department and join People Ops (what we call our human resources function) to manage this and other personal-growth programs. I am amused that Google lets an engineer teach emotional intelligence. What a company.

There turned out to be unexpected benefits to having an engineer like me teach a course like Search Inside Yourself. First, being very skeptical and scientifically minded, I would be deeply embarrassed to teach anything without a strong scientific basis, so Search Inside Yourself was solidly grounded in science. Second, having had a long career as an early engineer at Google, I had credible experience in applying emotional intelligence practices in my day job as I created products, managed teams, asked the boss for raises, and stuff. Hence, Search Inside Yourself had been stress-tested and applicable in daily life right out of the box. Third, my engineering-oriented brain helped me translate teachings from the language of contemplative traditions into language that compulsively pragmatic people like me can process. For example, where traditional contemplatives would talk about "deeper awareness of emotion," I would say "perceiving the process of emotion at a higher resolution," then further explaining it as the ability to perceive an emotion the moment it is arising, the moment it is ceasing, and all the subtle changes in between.

That is why Search Inside Yourself has the compelling features of being scientifically grounded, highly practical, and expressed in a language that even I can understand. See? I knew my engineering degree was good for something.

Search Inside Yourself has been taught at Google since 2007. For many participants, it has been life changing, both at work and in their personal lives. We receive a lot of post-course feedback similar to one that says, "I know this sounds melodramatic, but I really think this course changed my life."

At work, some participants have found new meaning and fulfillment in their jobs (we even had one person reverse her decision to leave Google after taking Search Inside Yourself!), while some have become much better at what they do. Engineering manager Bill Duane, for example, discovered the importance of giving himself quality time, so he reduced his working hours to four days a week. After he did that, he was promoted. Bill found time to take care of himself and discovered ways to accomplish more while doing less. I asked Bill about the most significant changes he experienced during Search Inside Yourself, and he said he learned to listen a lot better, gain control over his temper, and understand every situation better by, in his words, "learning to discern stories from reality." All these make him a much more effective manager to the benefit of the people working for him.

For Blaise Pabon, a sales engineer, Search Inside Yourself helped him become much more credible to customers because he is now better at calmly overcoming objections during product demonstrations, he speaks compassionately about competitors, and he is courageous and truthful when telling customers about our products. All these qualities earned him great respect among his customers. One engineer in the class found himself becoming much more creative after Search Inside Yourself. Another engineer told us that two of his most important contributions to his project came after doing mindfulness exercises he learned in Search Inside Yourself.

Not surprisingly, people found Search Inside Yourself to be even more beneficial in their personal lives. Many reported becoming significantly calmer and happier. For example, one participant said, "I have completely changed in the way I react to stressors. I take the time to think through things and empathize with other people's situations before jumping to conclusions. I love the *new me*!" Some have found the quality of their marriages improved. Others reported overcoming personal crises with the help of Search Inside Yourself. For example, one person told us, "I experienced personal tragedy—my brother's death—during the course of Search Inside Yourself, and [the class] enabled me to manage my grief in a positive way." One person simply said, "I now see myself and the world through a kinder, more understanding set of eyes."

This book is based on the Search Inside Yourself curriculum at Google. We saw how this knowledge and the practices enhanced creativity, productivity, and happiness in those who took the course. You will find many things in this book that are very useful for you, and some things that may even surprise you. For example, you will learn how to calm your mind on demand. Your concentration and creativity will improve. You will perceive your mental and emotional processes with increasing clarity. You will discover that self-confidence is something that can arise naturally in a trained mind. You will learn to uncover your ideal future and develop the optimism and resilience necessary to thrive. You will find that you can deliberately improve empathy with practice. You will learn that social skills are highly trainable and that you can help others love you.

What I find most rewarding is how well Search Inside Yourself has worked for ordinary folks in a corporate setting right here in a modern society. If Search Inside Yourself had worked this well for people from traditionally meditative cultures doing intensive retreats in zendos or something, nobody would be too surprised. But these are ordinary Americans working in a high-stress environment with real lives and families and everything, and still, they can change their lives in just twenty hours of classroom time spread over seven weeks.

Search Inside Yourself works in three steps:

1. Attention training
2. Self-knowledge and self-mastery
3. Creating useful mental habits

Attention Training

Attention is the basis of all higher cognitive and emotional abilities. Therefore, any curriculum for training emotional intelligence has to begin with attention training. The idea is to train attention to create a quality of mind that is calm and clear at the same time. That quality of mind forms the foundation for emotional intelligence.

Self-Knowledge and Self-Mastery

Use your trained attention to create high-resolution perception into your own cognitive and emotive processes. With that, you become able to observe your thought stream and the process of emotion with high clarity, and to do so objectively from a third-person perspective. Once you can do that, you create the type of deep self-knowledge that eventually enables self-mastery.

Creating Useful Mental Habits

Imagine whenever you meet anybody, your habitual, instinctive first thought is, *I wish for this person to be happy.* Having such habits changes everything at work, because this sincere goodwill is picked up unconsciously by others, and you create the type of trust that leads to highly productive collaborations. Such habits can be volitionally trained.

In creating Search Inside Yourself, we collected some of the best scientific data and gathered some of the best minds on the topic to create a curriculum that is proven to work. You will not want to miss this; it may change your life. Like, seriously.

I am confident that this book will be a valuable resource for you as you embark on your exciting journey. I hope your journey will be fun and profitable. And, yes, that it will contribute to world peace too.

CHAPTER ONE

Even an Engineer Can Thrive on Emotional Intelligence

What Emotional Intelligence Is and How to Develop It

What lies behind us and what lies ahead of us
are tiny matters to what lies within us.

—Ralph Waldo Emerson

I would like to begin our journey together on a note of optimism, partly because beginning on a note of pessimism does not sell books. More importantly, based on my team's experience teaching at Google and elsewhere, I am optimistic that emotional intelligence is one of the best predictors of success at work and fulfillment in life, and it is trainable for everyone. With the right training, anybody can become more emotionally intelligent. In the spirit of "if Meng can cook, so can you," if this training a highly introverted and cerebral engineer like me, it will prob-k for you.

"For some reason, Starfleet wants me to complete this course. You?"

The best definition of emotional intelligence comes from the two men widely regarded as the fathers of its theoretical framework, Peter Salovey and John D. Mayer. They define emotional intelligence as:

> *The ability to monitor one's own and others' feelings and emotions, to discriminate among them and to use this information to guide one's thinking and actions.*[1]

The groundbreaking book that popularized the topic is *Emotional Intelligence: Why It Can Matter More Than IQ,* written by Daniel Goleman, our friend and advisor. One of the most important messages in the book is that emotional competencies are not innate talents; they are learned abilities. In other words, emotional competencies are something you can deliberately acquire with practice.

Goleman adds a very useful structure to emotional intelligence by classifying it into five domains. They are:

1. Self-awareness: Knowledge of one's internal states, preferences, resources, and intuitions
2. Self-regulation: Management of one's internal states, impulses, and resources
3. Motivation: Emotional tendencies that guide or facilitate reaching goals
4. Empathy: Awareness of others' feelings, needs, and concerns
5. Social skills: Adeptness at inducing desirable responses in others

Salovey and Mayer are not the only people whose work relates to social and emotional intelligence. Howard Gardner, for example, famously introduced the idea of multiple intelligences. Gardner argued that people can be intelligent in ways not measured by an IQ test. A child, for example, may not be strong in solving math problems, but he may be gifted in language arts or composing music, and therefore we should consider him intelligent. Gardner formulated a list of seven intelligences (later increased to eight). Two of them, intrapersonal and interpersonal intelligences, are especially relevant to emotional intelligence. Gardner called them "personal intelligences." Goleman's five domains of emotional intelligence map very nicely into Gardner's personal intelligences: you can think of the first three domains of emotional intelligence as intrapersonal intelligence and the last two as interpersonal intelligence.

Funny enough, for me, the best illustration of emotional intelligence as a learned ability did not come from a scholarly publication but from the story of Ebenezer Scrooge in *A Christmas Carol.*[2] In the beginning of the story, Scrooge presents an example of low emotional intelligence. His intrapersonal intelligence is so low, he is incapable of creating emotional wellness for himself despite his wealth. In fact, his self-awareness is so bad, it takes three ghosts to help him figure himself out. His interpersonal intelligence is, of course, legendarily bad. Near the end of the story, however, Scrooge presents an example of elevated emotional intelligence. He develops strong self-awareness, he becomes capable of controlling his own emotional destiny, and his empathy and social skills blossom. Scrooge demonstrates that emotional intelligence is something that can be developed (in the version I saw, it happened in the space of a two-hour TV movie with enough time for commercials, but your mileage may vary).

Later in this book, we will examine the development of each domain of emotional intelligence in detail. Thankfully, it will not involve visits by Christmas ghosts.

Benefits of Emotional Intelligence

There is an important question that my friends in the training business call the so-what? question, as in, "Yes, very nice, but what can emotional intelligence do for me?" In the context of the work environment, emotional intelligence enables three important skill sets: stellar work performance, outstanding leadership, and the ability to create the conditions for happiness.

Stellar Work Performance

The first thing emotional intelligence enables is stellar work performance. Studies have shown that emotional competencies are twice as important in contributing to excellence as pure intellect and expertise.[3] A study by Martin Seligman, considered the father of modern positive psychology and the creator of the idea of learned optimism, showed that insurance agents who are optimists outsell their pessimist counterparts by 8 percent in their first year and 31 percent in their second year.[4] (Yes, I am optimistic about writing a bestseller. Thank you for asking.)

This was not surprising to me. After all, there are many jobs such as those in sales and customer service in which emotional competencies obviously make a big difference. We already know that intuitively. What surprised me was the report that this is true even for individual contributors in the tech sector, namely engineers like me whom you might expect to succeed purely on intellectual prowess. According to a study, the top six competencies that distinguish star performers from average performers in the tech sector are (in this order):

1. Strong achievement drive and high achievement standards
2. Ability to influence
3. Conceptual thinking
4. Analytical ability
5. Initiative in taking on challenges
6. Self-confidence[5]

Of the top six, only two (conceptual thinking and analytical ability) are purely intellectual competencies. The other four, including the top two, are emotional competencies.

Being strong in emotional intelligence can help everyone become outstanding at work, even engineers.

Outstanding Leadership

Emotional intelligence makes people better leaders. Most of us understand it intuitively based on our day-to-day experience interacting with those whom we lead and those who lead us. There are also studies that back up our intuition with scientific evidence. For example, Goleman reported an analysis that shows emotional competencies to make up to 80 to 100 percent of the distinguishing competencies of outstanding leaders.[6] This is illustrated by the story of Gerald Grinstein, a CEO who had to go through the painful process of cutting costs. Grinstein was tough, but being a virtuoso at interpersonal skills, he earned the cooperation of his employees and managed to keep their loyalty and spirits high while turning around their once-ailing company, despite having to make very tough decisions. In fact, Grinstein performed his magic not once but twice, once as CEO of Western Airlines and again as CEO of Delta. When Grinstein took over Delta amid a crisis, he immediately went about restoring lines of communication and trust within the company. He understood the importance of creating a positive work environment and, using extraordinary leadership skills (emotional intelligence), he turned a toxic work environment into a more family-like atmosphere.

Once again, I did not find any of this surprising, because we already intuitively understand the importance of emotional intelligence in leadership. What I found surprising was this is true even in the U.S. Navy. Another study by leadership expert Wallace Bachman showed that the most effective U.S. Navy commanders are "more positive and outgoing, more emotionally expressive and dramatic, warmer and more sociable (including smiling more), friendlier and more democratic, more cooperative, more likable and 'fun to be with,' more appreciative and trustful, and even gentler than those who were merely average."[7]

When I think of military leadership, I think of tough-as-nails people barking orders and expecting to be obeyed, so it is fascinating to me that even in a military environment, what distinguishes the best leaders from the merely average ones is emotional intelligence. The best military commanders are basically nice people who are fun to be with. Funny enough, the title of the Bachman study was "Nice Guys Finish First."

Nice Guys in the Military

The Ability to Create the Conditions for Happiness

Perhaps most importantly, emotional intelligence enables the skills that help us create conditions for our own sustainable happiness. Matthieu Ricard defines happiness as "a deep sense of flourishing that arises from an exceptionally healthy mind . . . not a mere pleasurable feeling, a fleeting emotion, or a mood, but an optimal state of being."[8] And that optimal state of being is "a profound emotional balance struck by a subtle understanding of how the mind functions."

In Matthieu's experience, happiness is a skill that can be trained. That training begins with deep insight into mind, emotion, and our experience of phenomena, which then facilitates practices that maximize our inner well-being at a deep level, ultimately creating sustainable happiness and compassion.

My own experience is similar to Matthieu's. When I was young, I was naturally very unhappy. If nothing good happened, then by default, I was unhappy. Right now, it is the reverse: if nothing bad happens, then by default, I am happy. I have become so naturally jolly that it even became part of my job title at Google: jolly good fellow. We all have a set point of happiness that we return to whenever the euphoria of a pleasant experience or the sting of an unpleasant experience fades out. Many of us assume this set point to be static, but my personal experience and that of many others like Matthieu suggest this set point to be movable with deliberate training.

Happily, the skills that help us cultivate emotional intelligence also help us identify and develop the inner factors that contribute to our deep sense of well-being. The same things that build emotional intelligence will also help us create conditions for our own happiness. Therefore, happiness may be an unavoidable side effect of cultivating emotional intelligence. Other side effects may include resilience, optimism, and kindness. (You may want to call your doctor to determine if happiness is right for you.)

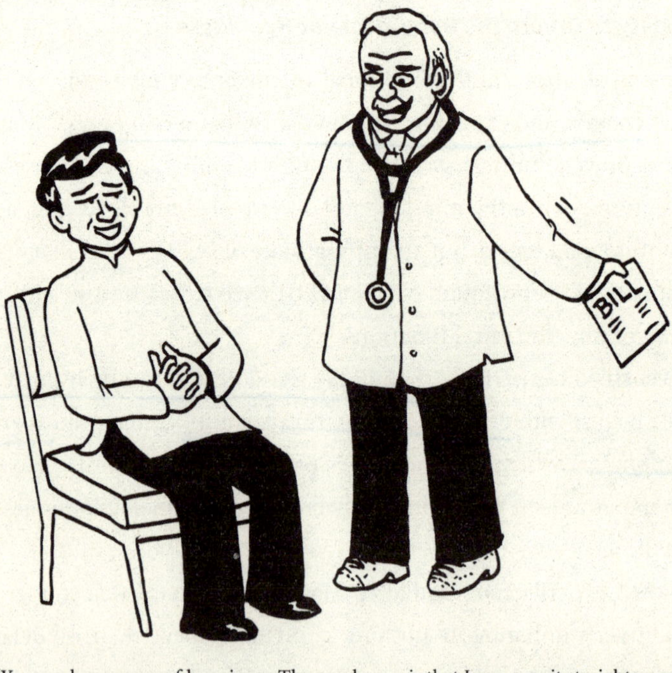

"Yes, you have a case of happiness. The good news is that I can cure it straightaway."

Truth be told, of the three good things enabled by emotional intelligence, happiness is the one I really care about. (Hush hush, but just between you and me and the million other people reading this book, the other points about stellar work performance and outstanding leadership, while useful and true and supported by scientific evidence, are used by me mostly to get a stamp of approval from upper management.) What I really care about is happiness for my co-workers. That is why emotional intelligence excites me. It doesn't just create the conditions for stellar success at work; it also creates the conditions for personal happiness for everyone. And I like happiness.

Optimize Thyself

If there is a one-word summary of everything I just said (hint: there is), that word is *optimize*. The aim of developing emotional intelligence is to help you optimize yourself and function at an even higher level than what you are already capable of. Even if you are already outstanding at what you do (which everybody in our class at Google is), sharpening and deepening your emotional competencies can give you an extra edge. We hope the training in these pages can help you go from good to great.

Cultivating Emotional Intelligence

When people come to a course such as ours that advertises itself as an "emotional intelligence course," most people expect it to be a purely behavioral course. They expect to be told how to play nice, share candy, and not bite their co-workers.

We decided on an entirely different approach, focusing primarily on expanding the range and depth of people's emotional abilities. We begin with the insight that emotional intelligence is a collection of emotional skills and, like all skills, emotional skills are trainable. We created a course to train those skills. We feel that if we develop skills, behavioral issues automatically go away. For example, if a person acquires the ability to skillfully manage his own anger, then all his behavioral issues involving anger are "automagically" solved. Emotional skillfulness frees us from emotional compulsion. We create problems when we are compelled by emotions to act one way or another, but if we become so skillful with our emotions that we are no longer compelled, we can act in rational ways that are best for ourselves and everybody else. And we will play nice, share candy, and not bite our co-workers.

Emotional intelligence is trainable, even in adults. This claim is based on a fairly new branch of science known as "neuroplasticity." The idea is that what we think, do, and pay attention to changes the structure and function of our brains. A very interesting example of this comes from drivers of traditional black cabs in London. To get a license to drive that cab, you need to navigate the twenty-five thousand streets of London and all its points of interest in your head. This is a difficult test that can take two to four years of intense training to prepare for. Research has shown that the part of the brain associated with memory and spatial navigation, the hippocampus, is bigger and more active in London cabbies than in the average person. More interestingly, the longer someone has been driving a cab in London, the larger and more active her hippocampus.[9]

One very important implication of neuroplasticity is that we can intentionally change our brains with training. For example, research by my friend and fellow Search Inside Yourself teacher Philippe Goldin shows that after just sixteen sessions of cognitive-behavioral therapy (CBT), people with social anxiety disorder are able to increase activity in the parts of their brains associated with self-regulation, linguistic processing, and attention when working with their own negative self-beliefs.[10] Think about it, if we can train our brains to overcome even serious emotional disorders, just imagine the possibility of using it to greatly improve the quality of our emotional lives. That is the promise of the science and practices described in these pages.

A fascinating example of the application of neuroplasticity comes from the work led by Christopher deCharms.[11] DeCharms had people who suffer from chronic pain lie inside a magnetic resonance imaging (MRI) scanner and, using real-time functional magnetic resonance imaging (rtfMRI) technology, he showed each participant an image of a fire on a video screen. The greater the neural activity in the parts of their brains associated with their pain, the greater the fire became. By using that visual display, he could get people to learn to up- or down-regulate that brain activity and, with that ability, participants reported a corresponding decrease in their levels of pain. He calls this "neuroimaging therapy."

Brain. Trainable. Good.

Train Attention

How do we begin training emotional intelligence? We begin by training **attention.** This may seem a little counterintuitive at first. I mean, what does attention have to do with emotional skills?

The answer is that a strong, stable, and perceptive attention that affords you calmness and clarity is the foundation upon which emotional intelligence is built. For example, self-awareness depends on being able to see ourselves objectively, and that requires the ability to examine our thoughts and emotions from a third-person perspective, not getting swept up in the emotion, not identifying with it, but just seeing it clearly and objectively. This requires a stable and clear, non-judging attention. Another example shows how attention relates to self-regulation. There is an ability called "response flexibility," which is a fancy name for the ability to pause before you act. You experience a strong emotional stimulus, but instead of reacting immediately as you normally would (for example, giving the other driver the bird), you pause for a split second, and that pause gives you choice in how you want to react in that emotional situation (for example, choosing not to give the other driver the bird, which may save you a lot of trouble because the other driver may be an angry old man with golf clubs who turns out to be the father of the woman you're dating). That ability depends again on having a quality of attention that is clear and unwavering.

To quote Viktor Frankl, "Between stimulus and response, there is a space. In that space lies our freedom and our power to choose our response. In our response lies our growth and our happiness." What a mind of calmness and clarity does is to increase that space for us.

The way to train this quality of attention is something known as "mindfulness meditation." *Mindfulness* is defined by Jon Kabat-Zinn as "paying attention in a particular way: on purpose, in the present moment, and non-judgmentally."[12] The famous Vietnamese Zen master Thich Nhat Hanh defined mindfulness very poetically as "keeping one's consciousness alive to the present reality,"[13] which I really like, but I found Jon's definition easier to explain to the engineers, and I like the engineers. Mindfulness is a quality of mind that we all experience and enjoy from time to time, but it is something that can be greatly strengthened with practice, and once it becomes sufficiently strong, it leads directly to the attentional calmness and clarity that forms the basis of emotional intelligence.

There is scientific evidence showing that improving our ability to regulate our attention can significantly impact how we respond to emotions. An interesting study by neuroimaging researcher Julie Brefczynski-

Lewis and colleagues revealed that when expert meditators (those with ten thousand or more hours of meditation training) were subjected to negative sounds (for example, a woman screaming), they showed lesser activation in the part of the emotional brain called the amygdala compared to novice meditators.[14] Furthermore, the more hours of meditation training the expert had, the lower the activation in the amygdala. This is fascinating because the amygdala has a privileged position in the brain—it is our brain's sentinel, constantly scanning everything we see for threats to our survival.

The amygdala is a hair trigger, which would rather be safe than sorry. When your amygdala detects what looks like a threat to your survival, such as a saber-toothed tiger charging at you or your boss slighting you, it puts you in a fight-flight-freeze mode and impairs your rational thinking. I find it fascinating that, simply with attention training, you can become good at regulating a part of the brain as primitive and important as the amygdala.

Another set of studies comes from the UCLA lab of Matthew Lieberman.[15] There is a simple technique for self-regulation called "affect labeling," which simply means labeling feelings with words. When you label an emotion you are experiencing (for example, "I feel anger"), it somehow helps you manage that emotion. Lieberman suggested the neural mechanisms behind how that process works. The evidence suggests that labeling increases the activity in the right ventrolateral prefrontal cortex (rVLPFC), commonly associated with being the brain's "brake pedal," which in turn increases the activation of part of the executive center of the brain called the medial prefrontal cortex (MPFC), which then downregulates the amygdala.

Another related study by David Creswell and Matthew Lieberman showed that for people strong in mindfulness, the neural process just described works even better and an additional part of the brain called the ventromedial prefrontal cortex (VMPFC) gets recruited as well. It suggests that mindfulness can help your brain utilize more of its circuitry, thereby making it more effective at managing emotions.[16]

Train at the Level of Physiology

Once we develop strong, stable, and perceptive attention, what do we do with it? We focus it on our bodies, of course. This again seems a little counterintuitive. What have our bodies got to do with developing emotional intelligence?

There are two very good reasons to work with our bodies: vividness and resolution.

Every emotion has a correlate in the body. Dr. Laura Delizonna, a researcher turned happiness strategist, very nicely defines emotion as "a basic physiological state characterized by identifiable autonomic or bodily changes."[17] Every emotional experience is not just a psychological experience; it is also a physiological experience.

We can usually experience emotions more vividly in the body than in the mind. Therefore, when we are trying to perceive an emotion, we usually get more bang for the buck if we bring our attention to the body rather than the mind.

More importantly, bringing the attention to the body enables a high-resolution perception of emotions. *High-resolution perception* means your perception becomes so refined across both time and space that you can watch an emotion the moment it is arising, you can perceive its subtle changes as it waxes and wanes, and you can watch it the moment it ceases. This ability is important because the better we can perceive our emotions, the better we can manage them. When we are able to perceive emotions arising and changing in slow motion, we can become so skillful at managing them, it is almost like living that cool scene in the movie *The Matrix*, in which Keanu Reeves's character, Neo, dodges bullets after he becomes able to perceive the moments the bullets are fired and see their trajectory in slow motion. Well, maybe we're not *that* cool, but you get the point. Unlike Neo, we're accomplishing our feat not by slowing down time, but by vastly upgrading our ability to perceive the experience of emotion.

The way to develop high-resolution perception of emotion is to apply mindfulness to the body. Using anger as the example, you may be able to train yourself to observe your mind all the time and then to catch anger as it arises in the mind. However, in our experience, it is far easier and more effective to do it in the body. For example, if your bodily correlate to anger is tightness in your chest, shallow breath, and tightness in your forehead, then when you're in an awkward social situation, the moment your chest tightens, your breath shallows, and your forehead tenses up, you know you are at the moment of arising anger. That knowledge gives you the ability to respond in ways of your own choosing (such as leaving the room before you do something you know you will regret, or choosing to allow the anger to bloom if that's the right response for the situation).

Essentially, because emotion has such a strong physiological component, we cannot develop emotional intelligence unless we operate at the level of physiology. That is why we direct our mindfulness there.

Last but not least, a useful reason to develop a high-resolution perception of the body is to strengthen our intuition. A lot of our intuition comes from our body, and learning to listen to it can be very fruitful. Here is an illustrative example from Malcolm Gladwell's book *Blink:*

> *Imagine that I were to ask you to play a very simple gambling game. In front of you are four decks of cards—two of them red and the other two blue. Each card in those four decks either wins you a sum of money or costs you some money, and your job is to turn over cards from any of the decks, one at a time, in such a way that maximizes your winnings. What you don't know at the beginning, however, is that the red decks are a minefield. . . . You can win only by taking cards from the blue decks . . . The question is how long will it take you to figure this out?*
>
> *A group of scientists at the University of Iowa did this experiment a few years ago, and what they found is that after we've turned over about fifty cards, most of us start to develop a hunch about what's going on. We don't know why we prefer the blue decks,*

but we're pretty sure, at that point, that they are a better bet. After turning over about eighty cards, most of us have figured the game out and can explain exactly why the first two decks are such a bad idea. But the Iowa scientists did something else, and this is where the strange part of the experiment begins. They hooked each gambler up to a polygraph—a lie detector machine—that measured the activity of the sweat glands that all of us have below the skin in the palms of our hands. Most sweat glands respond to temperature, but those in our palms open up in response to stress—which is why we get clammy hands when we are nervous. What the Iowa scientists found is that gamblers started generating stress responses to red decks by the tenth card, forty cards before they were able to say that they had a hunch about what was wrong with those two decks. More importantly, right around the time their palms started sweating, their behavior began to change as well. They started favoring the good decks.[18]

There may be a neurological explanation for why intuition is experienced in the body. Matthew Lieberman's review of research showed "evidence suggesting that the basal ganglia are the neuroanatomical bases of both implicit learning and intuition." The story behind basal ganglia is, once again, best told by our friend Daniel Goleman:

The basal ganglia observes everything we do in life, every situation, and extracts decision rules. . . . Our life wisdom on any topic is stored in the basal ganglia. The basal ganglia is so primitive that it has zero connectivity to the verbal cortex. It can't tell us what it knows in words. It tells us in feelings, it has a lot of connectivity to the emotional centers of the brain and to the gut. It tells us this is right or this is wrong as a gut feeling.[19]

That may be why intuition is experienced in the body and the gut, but it cannot be easily verbalized.

"Maybe you should concentrate more on developing the instinct part rather than the gut part."

From Mindfulness to Emotional Intelligence

Our approach to cultivating emotional intelligence begins with mindfulness. We use mindfulness to train a quality of attention that is strong both in clarity and stability. We then direct this power-charged attention to the physiological aspects of emotion so we can perceive emotion with high vividness and resolution. The ability to perceive the emotional experience at a high level of clarity and resolution builds the foundation for emotional intelligence.

And we live happily ever after.

In the upcoming chapters, we will explore this approach in more detail and then build additional skills on top of it to develop all five domains of emotional intelligence.

Mindfulness in Two Minutes

Most evenings, before we sleep, my young daughter and I sit in mindfulness together for two minutes. I like to joke that two minutes is optimal for us because that is the attention span of a child and of an engineer. For two minutes a day, we quietly enjoy being alive and being together. More fundamentally, for two minutes a day, we enjoy being. Just being. To *just be* is simultaneously the most ordinary and the most precious experience in life.

As usual, I let my experience with a child inform how I teach adults. This daily two-minute experience is the basis of how I introduce the practice of mindfulness in introductory classes for adults.

In learning and teaching mindfulness, the good news is that mindfulness is embarrassingly easy. It is easy because we already know what it's like, and it's something we already experience from time to time. Remember that Jon Kabat-Zinn skillfully defined mindfulness as "paying attention in a particular way: on purpose, in the present moment, and non-judgmentally." Put most simply, I think mindfulness is the mind of just being. All you really need to do is to pay attention moment-to-moment without judging. It is that simple.

The hard part in mindfulness practice is deepening, strengthening, and sustaining it, especially in times of difficulty. To have a quality of mindfulness so strong that every moment in life, even in trying times, is infused with a deep calmness and a vivid presence, is very hard and takes a lot of practice. But mindfulness per se is easy. It is easy to understand and easy to arise in ourselves. That ease is what I capitalize on as an instructor.

In my classes, after explaining some of the theory and brain science behind mindfulness, I offer two ways to experience a taste of mindfulness: the Easy Way and the Easier Way.

The creatively named Easy Way is to simply bring gentle and consistent attention to your breath for two minutes. That's it. Start by becoming aware that you are breathing, and then pay attention to the process of breathing. Every time your attention wanders away, just bring it back very gently.

The Easier Way is, as its name may subtly suggest, even easier. All you have to do is sit without agenda for two minutes. Life really cannot get much simpler than that. The idea here is to shift from "doing" to "being," whatever that means to you, for just two minutes. Just be.

To make it even easier, you're free to switch between the Easy Way and the Easier Way anytime during these two minutes. Any time you feel like you want to bring awareness to breathing, just switch to Easy. Any time you decide you'd rather just sit without agenda, just switch to Easier. No questions asked.

This simple exercise is mindfulness practice. If practiced often enough, it deepens the inherent calmness and clarity in the mind. It opens up the possibility of fully appreciating each moment in life, every one of which is precious. It is for many people, including myself, a life-changing practice. Imagine—something as simple as learning to just be can change your life.

Best of all, it is something even a child knows how to do. Oh, and an engineer too.

In the next chapter, we will take a deep dive into mindfulness.

"Like the man says, bro: Bee; just bee."

CHAPTER TWO

Breathing as if Your Life Depends on It

The Theory and Practice of Mindfulness Meditation

By non-doing, all doing becomes possible.

—Lao Zi

There is nothing mysterious about meditation. It's really just mental training.

The scientific definition of *meditation,* as suggested by Julie Brefczynski-Lewis, is "a family of mental training practices that are designed to familiarize the practitioner with specific types of mental processes."[1]

Brain Boot Camp

Traditional definitions of *meditation* are very close to the modern scientific one above. The Tibetan word for meditation is *Gom,* which means "to familiarize or to habituate." In Pali, the 2,600-year-old language of the earliest Buddhist texts, the word for meditation is *Bhavana,* which means "to cultivate," as in planting crops. Even in ancient societies with long meditation traditions, meditation was not seen as something magical or mysterious—it was just mental training. So if you come to meditation expecting magic, I'm very sorry; magic is three doors down the corridor.[2]

As the scientific definition of *meditation* above correctly suggests, there are many types of meditation designed to train different faculties of the mind. The specific type of meditation we are interested in for the purpose of developing emotional intelligence is mindfulness meditation, which was briefly introduced in the preceding chapter.

If meditation is about mental training, then what mental faculties does mindfulness train? Mindfulness trains two important faculties, **attention** and **meta-attention.** Attention is something we all understand. William James has a very nice definition for it: "taking possession by the mind, in clear and vivid form."[3]

Meta-attention is attention of attention, the ability to pay attention to attention itself. Huh? Simply put, meta-attention is the ability to know that your attention has wandered away. Let's say you are paying attention to an object, and eventually your attention wanders away to something else. After a while, there is something in your mind that "clicks" to let you know, hey, your attention has wandered. That faculty is meta-attention.

Meta-attention is also the secret to concentration. The analogy is riding a bicycle. The way you keep a bicycle balanced is with a lot of micro-recoveries. When the bike tilts a little to the left, you recover by adjusting it slightly to the right, and when it tilts a little to the right, you adjust it slightly to the left. By performing micro-recoveries quickly and often, you create the effect of continuous upright balance. It is the same with attention. When your meta-attention becomes strong, you will be able to recover a wandering attention quickly and often, and if you recover attention quickly and often enough, you create the effect of continuous attention, which is concentration.

Relaxed and Alert at the Same Time

The big secret of meditation, at least at the beginning stage, is it gets you to a state where your mind is relaxed and alert at the same time.

When your attention and meta-attention both become strong, something interesting happens. Your mind becomes increasingly focused and stable, but in a way that is relaxing. It is like balancing a bicycle on easy terrain. With enough practice, it becomes almost effortless and you get the experience of moving forward and being relaxed at the same time. You get where you need to be, and you actually enjoy the experience of getting there because it is relaxing.

With enough practice, you may even become able to bring your mind to that state on demand and stay in it for a prolonged period of time. When the mind becomes highly relaxed and alert at the same time, three wonderful qualities of mind naturally emerge: calmness, clarity, and happiness.

Here is the analogy. Imagine you have a pot of water full of sediments, and imagine that pot is constantly shaken and agitated. The water appears cloudy. Imagine that you stop agitating the pot and just let it rest on the floor. The water will become calm and, after a while, all the sediments will settle and the water will appear clear. This is the classical analogy of the mind in the alert and relaxed state. In this state, we temporarily stop agitating the mind the same way we stop agitating the pot. Eventually, our mind becomes calm and clear, the same way the water appears calm and clear.

Happiness Is the Default State of Mind

There is an extremely important quality of mind in the calm and clear state that is not captured by the above analogy. That quality is happiness. When the mind is calm and clear at the same time, happiness spontaneously arises. The mind becomes spontaneously and naturally joyful!

But why? Even after I found myself able to access that mind on demand, it did not make a lot of sense to me. Why should a calm and clear mind automatically be happy? I put that question to my friend Alan Wallace, one of the Western world's top experts in the practice of relaxed concentration (a practice known as *shamatha*).

Alan said the reason is very simple: **happiness is the default state of mind.** So when the mind becomes calm and clear, it returns to its default, and that default is happiness. That is it. There is no magic; we are simply returning the mind to its natural state.

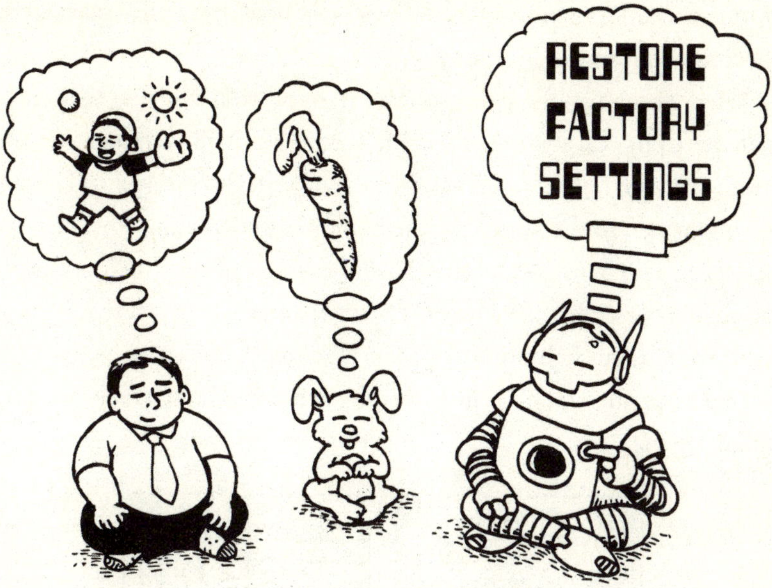

Happiness is the Default State of Mind

Alan, in his deep wisdom, said that in his usual calm, joyful, and understated manner. But to me, that statement represents a simple yet deeply profound, life-changing insight. It implies that happiness is not something that you pursue; it is something you allow. Happiness is just being. That insight changed my life.

To me, the biggest joke is that after all that has been done in the history of the world in the pursuit of happiness, it turns out that sustainable happiness is achievable simply by bringing attention to one's breath. Life is funny. At least my life is.

Meditation Is like Exercise

The traditional analogy of the pot of water filled with sediments is at least 2,600 years old. There is another analogy for meditation, which modern people may understand better, and that is the analogy of physical exercise. Meditation is exercise for the mind.

When you go to the gym, you are training your body so that it can gain more physical abilities. If you lift weights, you will eventually become stronger. If you regularly jog, your times will be faster and you will be able to run farther. In the same way, meditation is like training your mind so that it can gain more mental abilities. For example, if you do a lot of meditation exercises, your mind becomes calmer and more perceptive, you can focus your attention more strongly and for longer, and so on.

I joke that meditation is like sweating at the gym, minus the sweating, and the gym.

One important similarity between exercise and meditation is that, in both cases, growth comes from overcoming resistance. For example, when you are weight training, every time you flex your biceps in resistance to the weight of dumbbells, your bicep muscles grow a little bit stronger. The same process happens during meditation. Every time your attention wanders away from your breath and you bring it back, it is like flexing your biceps—your "muscle" of attention grows a bit stronger.

The implication of this insight is that there is no such thing as a bad meditation. For many of us, when we meditate, we find our attention wanders away from our breath a lot, and we keep having to bring it back, and then we think we're doing it all wrong. In fact, this is a good exercise because every time we bring a wandering attention back, we are giving our muscles of attention an opportunity for growth.

A second similarity between exercise and meditation is they can both significantly change the quality of your life. If you never exercise and you put yourself on a regular exercise regime, a few weeks or months later, you may find many significant changes in yourself. You will have more energy, you can get more stuff done, you get sick less often, you look better in the mirror, and you just feel great about yourself. The same is true for meditation. After a few weeks or months of starting a regular meditation regime, you have more energy; your mind becomes calmer, clearer, and more joyful; you get sick less; you smile more; your social life improves (because you smile more); and you feel great about yourself. And you don't even need to sweat.

Practice of Mindfulness Meditation

The process of mindfulness meditation is quite simple, as illustrated in the following diagram.

The process starts with an **intention.** Start by creating an intention, a reason for wanting to abide in mindfulness. Perhaps it is to reduce stress. Perhaps it is to increase your own well-being. Maybe you want to cultivate your emotional intelligence for fun and profit. Or maybe you just want to create the conditions for world peace, or something.

PROCESS MODEL OF MINDFULNESS MEDITATION

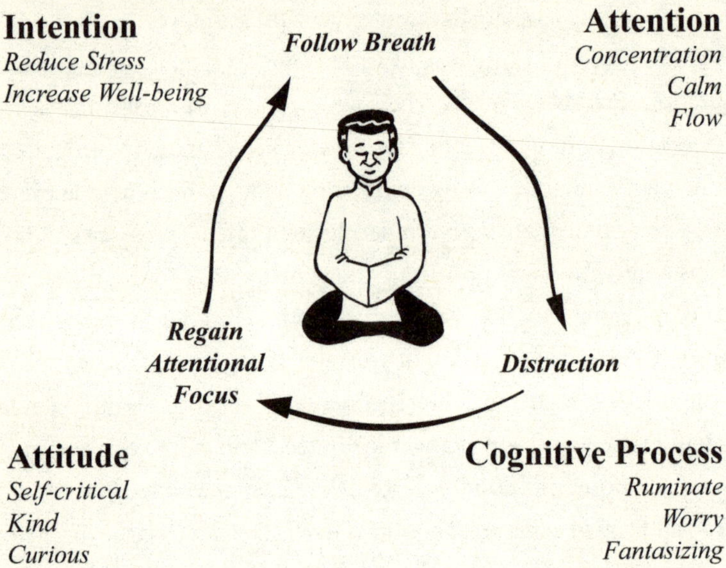

(Courtesy of Philippe Goldin)

In fact, if you are really lazy, or really busy, or really both, you can declare your meditation done right here. The act of creating good intentions is itself a form of meditation. Every time you create an intention, you are subtly forming or reinforcing a mental habit. If you create that same intention a lot, it eventually becomes a habit that will keep arising in your mind in varied situations to guide your behavior. For example, if many times a day you create the intention of caring for your own well-being, then after a while, in every situation you are in or with every decision you make, you may find yourself (perhaps unconsciously) biasing everything you do toward actions or decisions that increase well-being, and because of that, your well-being may actually improve.

This is even more powerful when your intention is toward the well-being of others. Just by forming that intention a lot, and not doing anything else, you may find yourself gradually (and, again, sometimes unconsciously) becoming kinder and nicer to other people. Pretty soon, many more people may like you and want to hang out with you, and you may not even know why—you may just think they are attracted to your good looks.

After creating the intention, the next thing to do is to **follow your breath.** Just bring a gentle attention to the process of breathing. That is all.

"Breath! *Breath*! I said follow *breath*!"

The classical analogy of this process is a guard standing at the city gates watching people go in and out of the city. He does not do anything; he only watches people go in and out with quiet vigilance. In the same way, you can think of your mind as a guard vigilantly watching your breath go in and out. You may pretend to have a big stick if it makes you feel cool. A really beautiful alternative analogy, suggested by my friend and fellow Search Inside Yourself teacher Yvonne Ginsberg, is a butterfly resting on the petal of a flower while the gentle breeze lifts and lowers it. Your attention is the butterfly and the petal is your breath.

At this point, your **attention** may gather. You may find yourself in a state where your mind is calm and concentrated. You may even be in the flow, just being with your breath. With enough practice, this state can last a long time, but for most people, this may go on for a few seconds. And then we fall into **distraction.**

In that state of distraction, we may start ruminating, worrying, or fantasizing. Sometimes, I even fantasize about not worrying. After a while, we realize our attention has wandered away. The default reaction of most people at this point is self-criticism. We start telling ourselves stories about how horrible we are as meditators and, by extension, not particularly good people either. Happily, there is a skillful way to deal with this.

The first thing to do is to simply **regain attentional focus** by bringing attention back to the process of breathing. The second thing to do is to remember an important insight we discussed earlier in this chapter—that this process of bringing a wandering attention back is like flexing your biceps during your gym workout. This is not failure; it is the process of growth and developing powerful mental "muscles."

The third thing to do is to become aware of your **attitude** toward yourself. See how you treat yourself and how often you engage in nasty gossip about yourself. If possible, shift the attitude toward self-directed kindness and curiosity. This shift is, by itself, another meditation. Once again, it is about forming mental habits.

Every time we create an attitude of self-directed kindness, we deepen that habit a little bit more, and if we do it a lot, we may overcome a lot of our self-hatred and even become our own best friend. (I am reminded of a very funny line in the movie *Space Balls,* "I'm a mog: half man, half dog. I'm my own best friend!")

One beautiful way of doing this is to create what the Zen folks call the "grandmother mind": adopting the mind of a loving grandmother. To a loving grandmother, you are beautiful and perfect in every way. No matter how much mischief you cause, you are perfect and Grandma loves you just as you are. It does not mean Grandma is blind to your faults, nor does it mean she allows you to hurt yourself. Sometimes, she even intervenes sternly to stop you from getting yourself into big trouble. But no matter what, you are perfect to her and she loves you.

The practice is to see yourself in the eyes of a loving grandmother.

And finally, return to following your breath and, whenever it is helpful, remind yourself of your intention. Welcome back.

Posture and Stuff

You can really meditate in any posture you want. Traditional Buddhism, for example, defines four main meditation postures: sitting, standing, walking, and lying down, which seems to cover just about everything. Those Buddhists are greedy.

When choosing a meditation posture for yourself, there is only one thing to remember. Just one. The best meditation posture is one that helps you remain **alert** and **relaxed** at the same time for a long period of time. That means, for example, you probably do not want a posture where you slouch, since that is not conducive to alertness, and you also do not want a posture that requires you to stiffen your back, since that is not conducive to relaxation.

Happily for us, a sitting posture optimized for both alertness and relaxation has already been developed over the thousands of years that people have been meditating. This traditional posture is sometimes called the seven-point meditation posture. In brief, the seven are:

1. Back straight "like an arrow"
2. Legs crossed in "lotus position"
3. Shoulders relaxed, held up and back, "like a vulture"
4. Chin tucked in slightly, "like an iron hook"
5. Eyes closed or gazing into space
6. Tongue held against the upper palate
7. Lips slightly apart, teeth not clenched

We do not have to go into details about the traditional posture. I found the formal forms of this posture to be initially difficult for most modern people because we do not sit on the floor much. Instead, we are so used to sitting on chairs or couches with backrests that the traditional posture feels a bit awkward for many of us, at least in the beginning. So my suggestion to you is just to be aware that a functionally optimized traditional posture exists. Use it as a guideline, and find whatever posture is comfortable for you and, most importantly, helps you remain alert and relaxed. For example, it does not really matter if you cross your legs or use a backrest, or if you really prefer a posture involving a Hello Kitty soft doll on your head. As long as you can remain alert and relaxed, that is good.

Sogyal Rinpoche, a world-renowned Tibetan Buddhist teacher, suggests a fun and useful way to find your own posture. He recommends sitting like a majestic mountain. The idea is to think of your favorite mountain, say Mount Fuji or Mount Kilimanjaro, and then pretend to be that mountain when you sit. And there you are, Mister (or Miss) Mount

Fuji, majestic, dignified, and awe inspiring. The nice thing is if you sit in a way that you feel majestic, dignified, and awe inspiring, it may also be the same posture that helps you become alert and relaxed, and it is kind of fun. Try this out and see if it works for you.

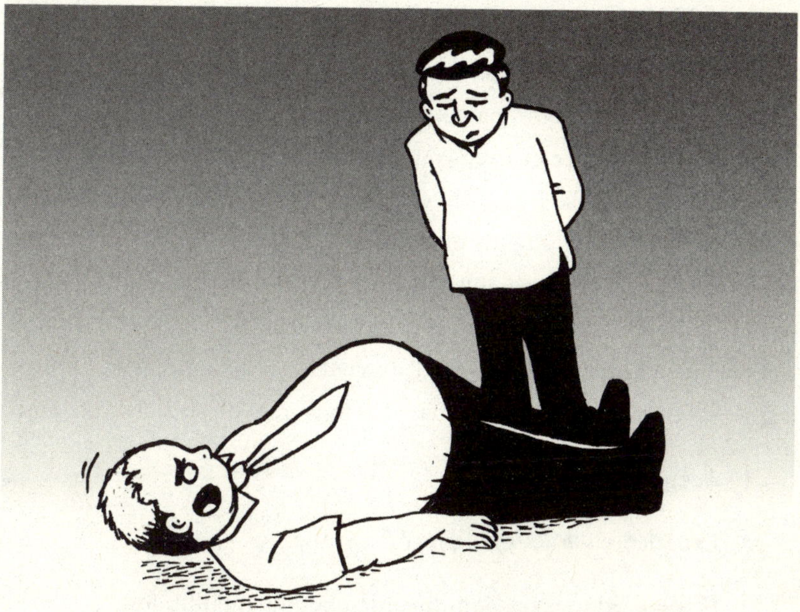

"But I more closely resemble a mountain with this posture."

Another simple but useful suggestion comes from Search Inside Yourself instructor Yvonne Ginsberg:

> *Take a deep breath, lifting the rib cage. Letting go of the breath, let the shoulders drop while the spine stays gently in place. Thus embodying the flow of a river and the stability of a mountain, simultaneously.*

One question I get asked a lot is whether your eyes should be open or closed when you meditate. The funny answer is: either, both, and neither. The real answer is, each has its upsides and downsides, so it is good to understand and play with the options.

Keeping your eyes closed during meditation is good; it helps you stay calm and keeps away visual distractions. The problem is it becomes easy to fall asleep. If you keep your eyes open, you have the reverse problem. You do not drift into sleep so easily anymore, but you get distracted by visual objects. What to do? What to do? There are two compromises, one temporal and one spatial.

The temporal compromise is to start with your eyes closed and then open them occasionally when you start drifting toward sleep. The spatial compromise is, if you can, keep your eyes half open. I like to joke that this is easy for me because I am Chinese. But really, the idea here is to open your eyes slightly, look slightly downward, and gaze at nothing in particular. In my own experience, this last option is the optimal one. I suggest trying each option out to see what works for you.

Often in our meditation, we get distracted by sounds, thoughts, or physical sensations. I suggest a four-step plan to work with such distractions:

1. Acknowledge.
2. Experience without judging or reacting.
3. If you need to react, continue maintaining mindfulness.
4. Let it go.

Acknowledge

Just acknowledge that something is happening.

Experience, Without Judging or Reacting

Whatever it is that you are experiencing, just experience it. Do not judge it to be good or bad. Let it be, let it be, as a famous song suggests. If it is possible, try not to react to it. If you have to react (for example, you really have to scratch), try to take five breaths before reacting. The reason to do this is to practice creating space between stimulus and reaction.

The more we are able to create space between stimulus and reaction, the more control we will have over our emotional lives. This skill that you develop here during sitting can be generalized to daily life.

If You Need to React, Continue Maintaining Mindfulness

If you need to react, for example you need to scratch or to stand up, maintain mindfulness over three things: intention, movement, and sensation. Remember that the goal of this practice is not keeping still; the goal is mindfulness. So as long as you maintain mindfulness, anything you do is fair game. This means, for example, that if you need to react to an itch on your face, first bring attention to the sensation of itching, then to the intention to scratch, and finally to the movement of your arm and finger and the sensation of scratching on your face.

Nothing more. Nothing less.

Let It Go

If it wants to be let go of, let it go. If not, just let it be.

Remember that letting go is not forcing something to go away. Instead, letting go is an invitation. We generously allow the recipient to choose whether or not to accept the invitation, and we are happy either way. When we let go of something that distracts our meditation, we are gently inviting it to stop distracting us, but we generously allow it to decide whether or not it wants to stay. If it decides to leave, that is fine. If it decides to stay, that is fine too. We treat it with kindness and generosity during its entire presence. This is the practice of letting go.

Finally, if you do not remember a single thing you read in this chapter so far (maybe because you do not care about this book but your wife made you sit down and read it), happily, Jon Kabat-Zinn has a one-phrase summary of this entire chapter:

> *Breathing as if your life depends on it.*

If you can only remember a single phrase in this chapter, remember this, and you will understand mindfulness meditation.

Sitting Time

Now that you have learned about the theory and practice of mindfulness meditation, let us now spend a few minutes sitting in mindfulness.

There are a number of ways you can do this. The simplest is just to extend the two-minute mindfulness exercise from the previous chapter. First, sit in a meditation posture that allows you to be alert and relaxed at the same time. Then whenever you are comfortable doing so, you may practice the Easy Way (which is to pay attention to the process of breathing and gently bringing attention back every time it wanders away), or the Easier Way (which is to sit without agenda and simply shift from doing to being). If you like, you may switch between Easy and Easier anytime. Do that for maybe ten minutes, or as long as you would like to. That will be your meditation practice.

If you prefer something more formal and structured, you can apply the Process Model of Mindfulness Meditation discussed earlier in this chapter. Start by sitting in a meditation posture that allows you to be alert and relaxed at the same time. Once you are comfortable, invite an intention to arise, one that is based on why you are sitting here, which will encourage you to continue your practice. Bring your attention to the process of breathing. If the mind is calm and concentrated, abide in that mind. If the mind gets distracted by a sound, a thought, or an itch, acknowledge the source of the distraction, experience it without judging it, and let it go if it wants to be let go. If you need to move, maintain mindfulness of intention, movement, and sensation. Gently bring your attention back to your breath. If self-criticism or self-judgment arises, invite a thought of self-directed kindness to arise, if it wants to. If not, just let it be; everything is fine. Do this for ten minutes, or as long as you would like to.

MINDFULNESS MEDITATION

Let us begin by sitting comfortably. Sit in a position that enables you to be both relaxed and alert at the same time, whatever that means to you. Or, if you prefer, you may sit like a majestic mountain, whatever that means to you.

Let us now take three slow, deep breaths to inject both energy and relaxation into our practice.

Now, let us breathe naturally and bring a very gentle attention to your breath. You can either bring attention to the nostrils, the abdomen, or the entire body of breath, whatever that means to you. Become aware of in breath, out breath, and space in between.

(Short pause)

If you like, you can think of this exercise as resting the mind on the breath. You can visualize the breath to be a resting place, or a cushion, or a mattress, and let the mind rest on it, very gently. Just be.

(Long pause)

(continued)

If at any time you feel distracted by a sensation, thought, or sound, just acknowledge it, experience it, and very gently let it go. Bring your attention very gently back to the breathing.

(Long pause)

If you like, let us end this meditation by inviting joyful inner peace to arise.

Breathing in, I am calm.

Breathing out, I smile.

This present moment,

Wonderful.

(Short pause)

Thank you for your attention.

Dude, Where Is the Science?

Meditation has at least one important thing in common with science: its heavy emphasis on the spirit of inquiry. In meditation, there are two aspects to the spirit of inquiry. First, a lot of meditation is about self-discovery. Yes, we start with training of attention, but attention is not the end goal of most meditation traditions; the true end goal is insight. The reason we create a powerful quality of attention is to be able to develop insights into the mind. Having a powerful attention is like having a powerful torchlight—it is fun to have, but its real purpose is to allow us to look inside the dark rooms of the mind and ourselves so that we can, well, search inside ourselves. And because it is ultimately about developing insight, the spirit of inquiry—at least of internal inquiry—has to be an essential component of one's meditation practice.

The second aspect of this spirit of inquiry extends beyond the internal and into the external world. Because meditators are so used to inquiry, we have also become very comfortable with science and scientific inquiry into meditation itself. This is true even for classically trained practitioners within ancient meditative traditions, such as Buddhism. To many of my friends, the most stunning example of this comfort with science was when the Dalai Lama said, "If scientific analysis were conclusively to demonstrate certain claims in Buddhism to be false, then we must accept the findings of science and abandon those claims."[4]

With this in mind, let us take a quick glance at some of the peer-reviewed scientific literature surrounding meditation.

One of the most telling of all research studies on meditation was conducted by two pioneers in the field of contemplative neuroscience, Richard Davidson and Jon Kabat-Zinn.[5] The study was eye-opening for many reasons. It was the first major study conducted in a business setting, with employees of a biotechnology company as subjects. This makes it highly relevant for somebody like me who operates in the corporate world. The study showed that after just eight weeks of mindfulness training, the anxiety level of the subjects was measurably lower, which is nice but not surprising, since the name of Jon Kabat-Zinn's training program is Mindfulness-Based Stress Reduction. If anxiety had not been measurably lower, it would have been quite awkward.

More surprisingly, when the electrical activity of the subjects' brains was measured, those in the meditation group showed significantly increased activity in the parts of their brains associated with positive emotions. The most fascinating finding had to do with their immune function. Near the end of the study, subjects were given flu shots, and those in the meditation group developed more antibodies to the influenza vaccine. In other words, after just eight weeks of mindfulness meditation, subjects were measurably happier (as measured in their brains) and showed a marked increase in developing immunity. Remember that this study was not conducted on bald guys wearing robes living in a monastery, but on ordinary people with real lives and real high-stress jobs in corporate America.

A later study conducted by Heleen Slagter, Antoine Lutz, Richard Davidson, et al., focused on attention.[6] Specifically, it explored meditation in relation to an interesting phenomenon known as "attentional-blink" deficit. There is a very simple way to explain attentional blink. Let's say you are shown a series of characters (either numbers or letters of the alphabet) on a computer screen one at a time, in quick succession (with about fifty milliseconds of delay between letters, which is half of one-tenth of a second). Let's say the entire series is made up of letters, except for two numbers. For example, let's say the series is P, U, H, 3, W, N, 9, T, Y. There are two numbers within the series of letters. Your task is to identify the two numbers.

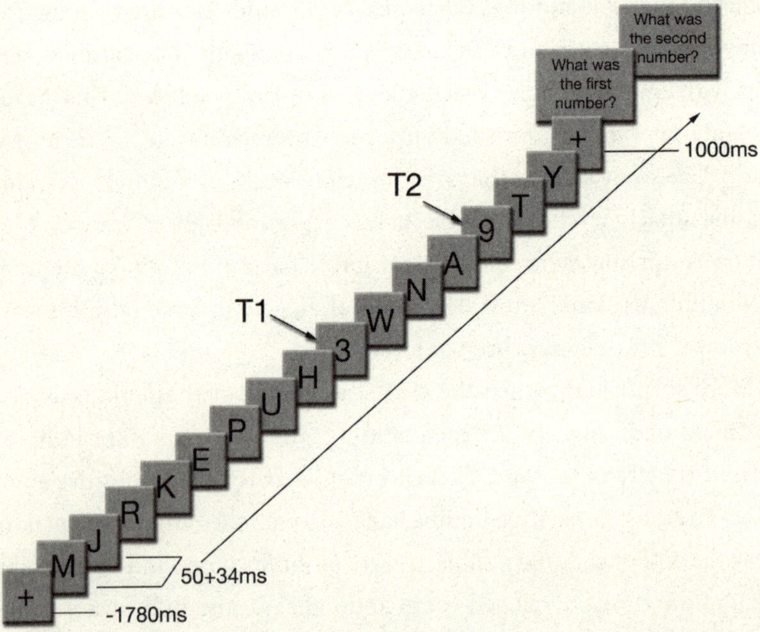

Attentional Blink Task

Here is the interesting part: if the two numbers are presented within half a second of each other, the second one is often not detected. This phenomenon is known as attentional blink. Somehow, after the first salient target is detected, mental attention "blinks," and it takes a while before the brain can detect the next one.

This attentional blink has previously been assumed to be a feature of our brain's wiring, and therefore, immutable. Slagter's study shows that after just three months of intensive and rigorous training in mindfulness meditation, participants can significantly reduce their attentional blink. The theory is that with mindfulness meditation training, one's brain can learn to process stimuli more efficiently, hence after processing the first salient target, it still has the mental resources to process the second.

This study is a fascinating glimpse into the possibility of upgrading the operating efficiency of our brains with mindfulness meditation. So if your job depends on your ability to pay attention to information for a prolonged period of time, maybe this meditation thing can help you get a raise.

"And you? You need a raise too? You're rising pretty good all by yourself!"

There are many more interesting scientific studies of meditation. We'll just point out a few more salient ones.

Antoine Lutz showed that adept Buddhist meditators are able to generate high-amplitude gamma brain waves, which are often associated with high effectiveness in memory, learning, and perception.[7] Better still, these adepts exhibit higher gamma-band activity even at baseline, when they are not meditating, suggesting that meditation training can change your brain at rest. If you pump iron a lot, you will have bulging muscles even when you are not working out in the gym. Similarly, when you do a lot of meditation training, you will have strong mental "muscles" of calmness, clarity, and joy even when you are just hanging out.

One early study in this field by Jon Kabat-Zinn revealed that mindfulness can greatly accelerate the healing of a skin condition known as psoriasis.[8] The methodology was simple. All participants were given the usual treatments, but for half of them, tapes of Jon Kabat-Zinn's meditation instructions were played to the participants during the treatment, and just playing the tapes significantly accelerated the healing process. While I find the results fascinating, what is compelling about this study is that psoriasis is something tangible and visible—a skin disease characterized by red spots that grow larger as they get worse. So when you talk about how meditation can help you heal in this context, it's not just woo-woo talk by some New Age person; it is something so tangible, you can see it and actually measure it with a ruler.

Finally, there is a study that suggests meditation can thicken your neocortex. This study, conducted by Sara Lazar, took MRI snapshots of mindfulness meditators and non-meditators, and showed that meditators have a thicker cortex in brain regions associated with attention and sensory processing.[9] Of course, these measurements show correlation, not causation, which means it is entirely possible that people with a thicker cortex in those brain regions just happen to be meditators. However, the study also showed that the longer the meditation subjects have been practicing meditation, the thicker those parts of their brains are, which suggests that meditation practice is causing those observed changes in the brain.

The above was just a snapshot of some of the research in the last twenty-five years. It is remarkable that mindfulness helps improve everything from attention and brain function to immunity and skin disease. Mindfulness feels almost like MacGyver's Swiss Army knife—it is useful in every situation.

Remember, if Meng can sit, so can you.

CHAPTER THREE

Mindfulness Without Butt on Cushion

Extending the Benefits of Mindfulness beyond Sitting

Mindfulness, I declare, is useful everywhere.

—Buddha

Mindfulness may be one of the most important things you can ever learn in your life. But don't take it from me. Here's what William James, the father of modern psychology, had to say:

> *And the faculty of voluntarily bringing back a wandering attention over and over again is the very root of judgment, character, and will. No one is* compos sui *if he have it not. An education which should*

> *improve this faculty would be* the *education* par excellence.[1] *(emphasis by original author)*

There you have it. Mindfulness is the skill that gives you the faculty of voluntarily bringing back a wandering attention over and over again, and as William James said, it is "*the* education *par excellence,*" the best thing you can learn. I hope that makes you feel better about spending money on this book.

In the previous chapter, we learned that mindfulness meditation is a key tool in developing emotional intelligence. In this chapter we will learn ways to extend mindfulness into every aspect of our daily lives. The mind of calmness and clarity you experience while sitting in mindfulness meditation is very nice, but it only becomes life changing when you can bring up that mind on demand, in day-to-day life. This chapter shows you how. I hope that makes you feel *really* good about spending money on this book.

"May I be excused from class? I've lost my mind."

In General, Generalize Mindfulness

One of the most important things a mindfulness meditator needs to do is extend the benefits of mindfulness beyond sitting into every part of life. During sitting meditation, you may experience some degree of calmness, clarity, and happiness, and the challenge is to generalize that mind into life situations outside formal sitting meditation.

The good news is the benefits of mindfulness training are already naturally generalizable or, put another way, easily incorporated into all areas of our lives. For example, your attention naturally gravitates toward things that are either very pleasant or very unpleasant, so if you can train yourself to keep your attention on something as neutral as your breath, then you can keep your attention on anything else. Your breath is like New York City for your attention—if your attention can make it here, it can make it anywhere. Hence, if you become very good at settling attention on breathing, you may find yourself able to pay much better attention in class or at meetings. Renowned meditation teacher Shaila Catherine told me that after she learned to meditate intensely during college, she never received any grade below an A.

That is the good news. The better news is there are things you can do to make your mindfulness training even more applicable to other areas of life.

There are two areas in which you can naturally and immediately start to integrate mindfulness. The first is to extend from mindfulness at rest to mindfulness during activity. The second is to extend from self-directed mindfulness to other-directed mindfulness. If you like, you can think of it as extending, or generalizing, mindfulness along two dimensions: one from rest to activity and the other from self to others. In the following few sections, I will suggest exercises for each.

Mindfulness in Activity

The best place to practice mindfulness is in daily life. Once you are able to bring mindfulness into every moment of daily life, your quality of life may change dramatically. Thich Nhat Hanh illustrates this beautifully with his description of the simple experience of walking:

> *People usually consider walking on water or in thin air a miracle. But I think the real miracle is not to walk either on water or in thin air, but to walk on earth. Every day we are engaged in a miracle which we don't even recognize: a blue sky, white clouds, green leaves, the black, curious eyes of a child—our own two eyes. All is a miracle.*[2]

When in mindfulness, even the simple experience of walking on earth can be a beautiful miracle.

In my own experience, mindfulness can increase my happiness without changing anything else. We take for granted many of the neutral things in life, such as not being in pain, having three meals a day, and being able to walk from point A to point B. In mindfulness, these become causes of joy because we no longer take them for granted. In addition, pleasant experiences become even more pleasant because our attention is there to fully experience them. For example, a delicious meal when consumed in mindfulness becomes more enjoyable simply because you put your full attention into enjoying the meal. When living in mindfulness, neutral experiences tend to become pleasant, and pleasant experiences become more pleasant. There is no cost or downside (nor down payment). What a great deal.

Once, when I was quite young, my father took the family to an expensive Chinese restaurant and ordered some of the signature dishes. During the meal, I caught myself giving the experience my full attention, partly because the meal was indeed very tasty, partly because it was so expensive, and partly because I considered it a fairly rare experience. It wasn't every day that we splurged on food. Because of all that, I found myself deep in mindfulness during the meal. And then it occurred to me, why did I have to be this mindful only during expensive meals? What if I pretended that every meal was rare and expensive, and gave it as much attention as I could? I call it the Expensive Food Meditation. I have been practicing it at most meals ever since, which is kind of ironic since I eat most of my meals at Google and food at Google is free.

If you have no other practice but sitting, the mindfulness will eventually grow into daily life and give you a no-cost, zero-down-payment happiness boost. However, you can accelerate this generalization process by purposefully bringing mindfulness to activity. The simplest way to do it is to bring full moment-to-moment attention to every task with a nonjudgmental mind, and every time attention wanders away, just gently bring it back. It is just like sitting meditation, except the object of meditation is the task at hand rather than the breath. That is all.

For those who prefer a more formal practice, the best such practice I know of is walking meditation. The nice thing about formal walking meditation is that it has the dignity, focus, and rigor of sitting meditation, but it is done in motion and necessarily with eyes opened (otherwise, it will become bumping-into-people-and-things meditation), so it is highly conducive to bringing the mental calmness of sitting meditation into activity. In fact, this is such a useful practice that in many formal meditation trainings, students are asked to alternate between sitting and walking meditation.

Walking meditation is really as simple as it sounds. When walking, bring full moment-to-moment attention to every movement and sensation in the body, and every time attention wanders away, just gently bring it back.

WALKING MEDITATION

Start by standing still. Bring attention to this body. Become aware of the pressure on the feet as they touch the ground. Take a moment to experience this body standing on the ground.

(continued)

Now, take a step forward. Lift one foot mindfully, move it forward mindfully, plant it down in front of you mindfully, and shift your weight to this foot mindfully. Take a short pause, and do it with the other foot.

If you like, when lifting your foot, you may repeat silently to yourself, "Lifting, lifting, lifting," and when moving and planting your foot forward, you may repeat silently to yourself, "Moving, moving, moving."

After taking a number of steps, you may wish to stop and turn around. When you decide to stop, just take a few seconds to become mindful of your body in a standing position. If you like, you may repeat silently to yourself, "Standing, standing, standing." As you turn around, do it mindfully, and if you like, you may repeat silently to yourself, "Turning, turning, turning."

If you wish, you may synchronize your movement with your breathing. When lifting your foot, breathe in, and when moving and planting your foot, breathe out. Doing this may help inject calmness into the experience.

You do not have to walk slowly when doing walking meditation; it can be done at any speed. This means you can do walking meditation every time you walk.

For myself, I do it every time I walk from my office to the restroom and back. I found mindful walking to be restful for the mind, and a relaxed mind is conducive to creative thinking. Hence, I find this very useful for my work, which often requires some creative problem solving, so every time I take a restroom break, my mind gets the opportunity to rest into a creative state. Problems often get solved in my mind during my restroom breaks. (Yes, I seem most productive during breaks, so maybe my employer should pay me to take breaks. Boss, I hope you are reading this.)

It is advantageous for us that pacing is accepted in our culture. It means you can do walking meditation any time of the day, and people will think you are just pacing. You do not even have to wait for restroom breaks to do walking meditation.

Dog-Walking Meditation

Other-Directed Mindfulness

A beautiful way to practice mindfulness, which is almost guaranteed to improve your social life, is to apply mindfulness toward others for the benefit of others. The idea is very simple—give your full moment-to-moment attention to another person with a nonjudgmental mind, and every time your attention wanders away, just gently bring it back. It is just like the meditation we have been practicing, except the object of meditation is the other person.

You can practice mindful listening either formally or informally. The formal practice involves creating an artificial environment for one person to speak while another listens mindfully. The informal practice is to listen mindfully to another person and generously give him or her the space to speak during any ordinary conversation.

FORMAL PRACTICE OF MINDFUL LISTENING

In this exercise, we will practice listening in a way that is different from how we usually listen.

We will do this in pairs, with a family member or a friend, each person taking turns to be the speaker and the listener.

Instructions for the speaker: This will be a monologue. You get to speak uninterrupted for 3 minutes. If you run out of things to say, that is fine; you can just sit in silence and whenever you have something to say, you may continue speaking again. The entire 3 minutes belong to you, you can use the time in whatever ways you want, and know that whenever you are ready to speak, there is a person ready to listen to you.

Instructions for the listener: Your job is to listen. When you listen, give your full attention to the speaker. You may not ask questions during these 3 minutes. You may acknowledge with facial expressions, by nodding your head, or by saying, "I see," or "I understand." You may not speak except to acknowledge. Try not to over-acknowledge, or you might end up leading the speaker. And if the speaker runs out of things to say, give her the space for silence, and then be available to listen when she speaks again.

Let us have one person speak and one listen for 3 minutes and then switch over for another 3 minutes. After that, have a 3-minute meta-conversation, in which both of you talk about what this experience was like for you.

Suggested topics for the monologue:

- What are you feeling right now?
- What is something that happened today that you want to talk about?
- Anything else you want to talk about.

INFORMAL PRACTICE OF MINDFUL LISTENING

When a friend or loved one is speaking to you, adopt a generous attitude by giving this person the gift of your full attention and the gift of airtime. Remind yourself that because this person is so valuable to you, he or she is entitled to all your attention and all the space and time needed to express himself or herself.

As you listen, give your full attention to the speaker. If you find your attention wandering away, just very gently bring it back to the speaker, as if he or she is a sacred object of meditation. As much as possible, try to refrain from speaking, asking questions, or leading the speaker. Remember, you are giving him or her the valuable gift of airtime. You may acknowledge with facial expressions, or by nodding your head, or by saying, "I see," or "I understand," but try not to over-acknowledge so as to not lead the speaker. If the speaker runs out of things to say, give him or her space for silence, and then be available to listen when he or she speaks again.

When we do formal practice in class, the most common feedback is people really appreciate being listened to. We often do the formal exercise at the beginning of our seven-week Search Inside Yourself course, in which most participants start out not knowing each other. We frequently hear people telling us right after this exercise, "I got to know this person for six minutes, and we are already friends. Yet there are people who have been sitting in the next cubicle for months, and I don't even know them." This is the power of attention. Just giving each other the gift of total attention for six minutes is enough to create a friendship. My friend and fellow Search Inside Yourself teacher, the Zen master Norman Fischer said, "Listening is magic: it turns a person from an object outside, opaque or dimly threatening, into an intimate experience, and therefore into a friend. In this way, listening softens and transforms the listener."[3]

Our attention is the most valuable gift we can give to others. When we give our full attention to somebody, for that moment, the only thing in the world that we care about is that person, nothing else matters because nothing else is strong within our field of consciousness. What can possibly be a more valuable gift than that? As usual, Thich Nhat Hanh put it most poetically: "The most precious gift we can offer others is our presence. When mindfulness embraces those we love, they will bloom like flowers."[4]

If there are people in your life you care about, be sure to give them a few minutes of your full attention every day. They will bloom like flowers.

"I'm getting his full attention all right, but I don't think I'm blooming."

Mindful Conversation

We can extend mindful listening into the extremely useful practice of **mindful conversation.** This practice came to us from our friends in the legal community and is especially useful in mediation. Specifically, master mediator Gary Friedman taught it to Zen master Norman Fischer, who in turn taught it to us at Google.

There are three key components to mindful conversation. The first and most obvious one is mindful listening, which we have already practiced.

The second is something Gary called **"looping,"** short for "closing the loop of communication." Looping is simple. Let's say there are two people involved in this conversation—Allen and Becky—and it is Allen's turn to speak. Allen speaks for a while, and after he is done speaking, Becky (the listener) loops back by saying what she thought she heard Allen say. After that, Allen gives feedback on what he thought was missing or misrepresented in Becky's characterization of his original monologue. And they go back and forth until Allen (the original speaker) feels satisfied that he is correctly understood by Becky (the original listener). Looping is a collaborative project in which both people work together to help Becky (the listener) fully understand Allen (the speaker).

The third key component to mindful conversation is something Gary called **"dipping,"** or checking in with ourselves. The main reason we do not listen to others is that we get distracted by our own feelings and internal chatter, often in reaction to what the other person said. The best way to respond to these internal distractions is to notice and acknowledge them. Know that they are there, try not to judge them, and let them go if they are willing to go. If feelings or other internal distracters decide to stay around, let them be and just be aware of how they may affect your listening. You can think of dipping as self-directed mindfulness during listening.

Dipping is also useful for the speaker. As the speaker speaks, it is useful for her to dip and see what feelings arise as she is speaking. If she likes, she may talk about them, or if she prefers, simply acknowledge them, try not to judge them, and let them go if they are willing to go.

Our class participants often ask how we can give our full attention to somebody speaking and dip at the same time. The analogy we give is peripheral vision. When we are looking at something, we have central vision and peripheral vision. We can see the chosen object clearly (with central vision), and at the same time, we have a visual sense of what is around it (using peripheral vision). Similarly, we can think of our attention as having a central component and a peripheral component, so we can give our central attention to the other person for listening and still maintain a peripheral attention to ourselves for dipping.

You can practice mindful conversation either formally or informally. The formal practice involves creating an artificial environment for each person to practice the three techniques of listening, looping, and dipping. The informal practice is simply to use those techniques in everyday conversation.

FORMAL PRACTICE OF MINDFUL CONVERSATION

The three parts to this skill are listening, looping, and dipping. Listening means giving the gift of attention to the speaker. Looping means closing the loop of communication by demonstrating that you have really heard what the person is saying. Do not try to remember everything: if you really listen, you will hear. Dipping means checking in with yourself, knowing how you are feeling about what you are hearing. Part of the practice is becoming able to give full attention to the speaker, with full awareness of your own feelings.

Instructions

Part I: Monologue

Person A speaks in monologue for 4 minutes. When you are speaking, maintain some mindfulness on your body (this is the dipping part). The entire 4 minutes belong to you, so if you run out of things to say, you can both sit in silence, and when you have something else to say later, you may just say it.

Person B listens. Your job is to give your full attention to the speaker as a gift, while at the same time maintaining some mindfulness on your body (this is again the dipping part). You are giving him the gift of your attention, without losing awareness of your body. You may acknowledge, but do not over-acknowledge. You may not speak except to acknowledge.

Part II: Resolution

After that, B repeats back to A what she thinks she heard. B may start by saying, "What I heard you say was . . ." Immediately after, A gives feedback by telling B what he feels B got right or wrong (for example, what she missed, what she misrepresented, etc). Go back and forth until A is satisfied that he is completely understood by B. Do this for as long as it takes, or until 6 minutes are up. (This is the looping part).

Then we switch places, so B gets to be the speaker and A the listener.

After the exercise, spend 4 minutes in meta-conversation discussing the experience.

Some suggested topics for conversation:

- Your self-assessment. Your impressions of yourself, what you like, what you want to change, etc.
- A difficult situation that happened recently or a long time ago that you want to talk about.
- Any other topic that is meaningful to you.

You can think of the informal practice of mindful conversation as the stealthy version of the formal practice. You do not have to tell your friend, "Hey, I want to try out this practice I read from a really nice book, so I'm going to loop you and dip myself." That may be awkward. Instead, you can just say, "What you say sounds important. To make sure I understand you correctly, I would like to repeat to you what I think I heard. Let me know if my understanding is correct. Is that okay for you?" Most likely, your friend will really appreciate that because you are taking the time and trouble to listen and to understand him or her correctly. In making this request, you are implicitly demonstrating that you value and respect your friend.

This is very beneficial for relationships.

INFORMAL PRACTICE OF MINDFUL CONVERSATION

You can practice mindful conversation during any conversation, but it is most useful when communication is at an impasse, for example, in a conflict situation.

The three parts to this skill are listening, looping, and dipping. Listening means giving the gift of attention to the speaker. Looping means closing the loop of communication by demonstrating that you have really heard what the person is saying. Dipping means checking in with yourself, knowing how you are feeling about what you are hearing.

Begin with mindful listening (see page 59). Give the speaker the gift of your attention without losing awareness of your body. If any strong emotion arises, acknowledge it and, if possible, let it go. After the speaker is done expressing her views, make sure you fully understood by asking for permission to repeat back what you heard. You may say something like, "What you say sounds important. To make sure I understand you correctly, I would like to repeat to you what I think I heard. Let me know if my understanding is correct. Is that okay for you?" If the speaker says yes, repeat back what you heard and then invite the speaker to let you know what you understood correctly or incorrectly. After the speaker offers her input, repeat her corrections in your own words to make sure you understood those correctly. Repeat this process until the speaker is fully satisfied that she is understood.

After demonstrating that you understood the speaker, it is your turn to speak. If you are comfortable doing so, you may explain the looping process and respectfully invite the other person to participate if she wants to. You may say something like, "I want to make sure I do not miscommunicate anything, so if it is okay with you, after I speak, I'd like to invite you to let me know what you heard. Shall we do that?" If the other person accepts the invitation, you may apply the looping process.

Sustaining Your Practice

We have discussed mindfulness practices for developing a quality of mind that is calm and clear at the same time, and practices for extending that mindfulness into everyday situations. The keyword is *practice.* Mindfulness is like exercise—it is not sufficient to just understand the topic; you can only benefit from it with practice.

As an instructor, I found it fairly easy to get people started on mindfulness practice. I usually just need to show them the brain science, explain the benefits, introduce a short two-minute sitting, and voilà, people get it. That is the good news.

The bad news is after the first few days, many people find it hard to sustain the practice. Many of us start the first few days with great enthusiasm, committing ourselves to ten or twenty minutes a day of this wonderful practice, but after that initial enthusiasm, it starts to feel like a chore. You sit there bored and restless, wondering why time goes by so slowly, and then after a while, you decide you have more important and/or interesting things to do, such as getting stuff done or watching cats flush toilets on YouTube. And before you know it, you have lost your daily practice. One person who has a funny way of describing this state is the Tibetan meditation master His Eminence the Very Venerable Yongey Mingyur Rinpoche (but hey, call him Mingyur, he insists). Talking about himself as a very young beginner, he said, "Although I liked the idea of meditation, I didn't like the practice of meditation."

How can we sustain a mindfulness practice?

Happily, the difficulty of sustaining a mindfulness practice often lasts only a few months. It is like starting an exercise regime. The first few months are usually really hard—you probably have to discipline yourself into exercising regularly, but after a few months, you find your quality of life changing dramatically. You have more energy, you suffer fewer sick days, you can get more stuff done, and you look better in the mirror. You feel great about yourself. Once you reach that point, you just cannot

not do it anymore. The upgrade in quality of life is just too compelling. From that point on, your exercise regime becomes self-sustaining. Yes, you probably still have to cajole yourself into the gym every now and then, but it becomes fairly easy.

It is the same with sustaining a mindfulness practice. You probably need some discipline in the beginning, but after a few months, you may notice dramatic changes in quality of life. You become happier, calmer, more emotionally resilient, more energetic, and people like you more because your positivity emanates onto them. You feel great about yourself. And again, once you reach that point, it is so compelling, you just cannot not practice anymore. Yes, even a seasoned meditator needs to cajole herself onto the cushion every now and then, but it becomes fairly easy and habitual.

So how do you sustain your practice up to the point it becomes so compelling that it is self-sustaining? We have three suggestions:

1. Have a buddy: We learned this from Norman Fischer, whom we jokingly call the Zen abbot of Google. Once again, we use the gym analogy. Going to the gym alone is hard, but if you have a gym buddy with whom you commit to going, you are much more likely to go regularly. This is partly because you have company and partly because this arrangement helps you encourage each other and hold each other accountable (what I jokingly call mutual harassment).

   We suggest finding a mindfulness buddy and committing to a fifteen-minute conversation every week, covering at least these two topics:

   - How am I doing with my commitment to my practice?
   - What has arisen in my life that relates to my practice?

   We also suggest ending the conversation with the question, how did this conversation go? We instituted this in Search Inside Yourself and found it very effective.

2. Do less than you can: This lesson came from Mingyur Rinpoche. The idea is to do less formal practice than you are capable of. For example, if you can sit in mindfulness for five minutes before it feels like a chore, then do not sit for five minutes—just do three or four minutes, perhaps a few times a day. The reason is to keep the practice from becoming a burden. If mindfulness practice feels like a chore, it's not sustainable. Yvonne Ginsberg likes to say, "Meditation is an indulgence." I think her insight beautifully captures the core of Mingyur's idea.

   Do not sit for so long that it becomes burdensome. Sit often, for short periods, and your mindfulness practice may soon feel like an indulgence.

3. Take one breath a day: I may be the laziest mindfulness instructor in the world because I tell my students all they need to commit to is one mindful breath a day. Just one. Breathe in and breathe out mindfully, and your commitment for the day is fulfilled; everything else is a bonus.

   There are two reasons why one breath is important. The first is momentum. If you commit to one breath a day, you can easily fulfill this commitment and can then preserve the momentum of your practice. Later, when you feel ready for more, you can pick it back up easily. The second reason is creating the intention to meditate is itself a meditation.

   This practice encourages you to generate an intention to do something kind and beneficial to yourself daily, and over time, that self-directed kindness becomes a valuable mental habit. When self-directed kindness is strong, mindfulness becomes easier.

   Remember, one breath a day for the rest of your life. That is all I ask.

Lightness and Joy in Meditation

When I was new to meditation, I struggled with the simplest and silliest of all problems: I could not breathe. I mean, I could take in air and all during the normal course of the day, but when I tried consciously bringing my attention to my breath, I could not breathe properly. I was trying too hard.

One day, I decided I was going to stop trying hard. I was just going to sit, smile, and take note of my body while I sat, that was all. After just a few minutes of doing that, I fell into the state where I became alert and relaxed at the same time. And then I caught myself breathing normally. That was the first time I was able to pay attention to my breath and breathe properly at the same time. Only by not trying did I finally succeed. If I were a TV character, I would have looked up at the sky at that moment and sarcastically said, "Very funny."

In a humorous way, meditation is like trying to fall asleep. The more relaxed you are, the less you are fixated on the goal, the easier it becomes, and the better the outcome. The reason for this is that meditation and falling asleep have one important feature in common: they both rely on letting go.

The better you are at letting go, the better you are at both meditating and falling asleep. That is why many meditation teachers tell their students to have no expectations about their practice, because being fixated on outcomes interferes with the letting-go mind. I think this approach is correct, but it creates a vexing problem: if people have no expectation of benefits, why would they want to practice at all?

The best solution I know was suggested by Alan Wallace: "Have expectations before meditation, but have no expectation during meditation."[5] Solved. Simple, elegant solutions like this one warm the hearts of little old engineers like me.

Having a relaxed mind is very useful in meditation. Relaxation is the foundation of deep concentration. When the mind is relaxed, it becomes more calm and stable. These qualities in turn strengthen relaxation, thus forming a virtuous cycle. Paradoxically, deep concentration is built upon relaxation.

A similar mechanism works in the practice of mindfulness. I found lightness to be highly conducive to mindfulness. Lightness gives rise to ease of mind. When the mind is at ease, it becomes more open, perceptive, and nonjudgmental. These qualities deepen mindfulness, which in turn strengthens lightness and ease, thus forming a virtuous cycle of deepening mindfulness.

This insight suggests that a really good way to practice mindfulness is **using joy as an object of meditation,** especially the type of joy with a gentle quality that doesn't overwhelm the senses. For example, taking a nice walk, holding hands with a loved one, enjoying a good meal, carrying a sleeping baby, or sitting with your child while she is reading a good book are great opportunities to practice mindfulness by bringing full moment-to-moment attention to the joyful experience, to the mind, and to the body. I call it Joyful Mindfulness.

The first effect of bringing mindfulness to joyful experiences is they become even more enjoyable, simply because you are more present to enjoy them—extra enjoyment at no additional cost. More importantly, I found this mindfulness gain to be generalizable. That means if you practice and strengthen mindfulness during joyful experiences, that gain in mindfulness infuses other experiences as well, so you end up with stronger mindfulness in neutral and unpleasant experiences too. (Having fun as a meditation, what a great deal!)

Having said that, it is important to note that Joyful Mindfulness is best practiced as a complement to, not a replacement for, formal sitting practice. Formal practice requires you to bring mindfulness to neutral experiences like your breath, and because attention naturally gravitates away from neutral experiences, that mindfulness gain is a lot more generalizable. So comparing formal sitting to Joyful Mindfulness, you find that the former gives you better mindfulness gain, but unfortunately, requires discipline, and discipline is a scarce resource. In contrast, Joyful Mindfulness gives you less mindfulness gain but is far more sustainable. Plus, it is fun, and nobody can argue with fun—I know I can't. Hence, you can think of Joyful Mindfulness as the first gear of a car: it can easily move the car, but if you only use the first gear, you cannot go fast. In contrast, think of formal sitting as the higher gears: it is harder to get a stationary car to move using those gears, but they are the ones that get you good speed and mileage.

These two practices turn out to complement each other very well. Doing both practices every day is like making use of the full set of gears in your car: you can start the car moving smoothly and get a good speed.

More importantly, after a while, your formal meditation may be infused with a powerful quality known in Sanskrit as *sukha.* The most common translations for *sukha* are "bliss," "ease," and "happiness." In my opinion, the best translation of *sukha* is its most technical translation: "non-energetic joy." Sukha is a quality of joy not requiring energy. It is almost like white noise in the background, something that is always there but seldom noticed. There are two important implications of sukha's non-energetic quality. The first is that it is highly sustainable because it does not require exertion of energy. The second is that because it does not require energy, it is so subtle that it takes a very quiet mind to access, like a soft background hum that is audible only when nobody in the room is talking loudly. What that means is you need to learn to quiet your mind to access sukha, but once you become skillful at doing that, you have a highly sustainable source of happiness that does not require sensual input. Talk about life changing.

Almost all seasoned meditators I know arrive at sukha at some point in their meditative careers. However, my own experience suggests that Joyful Mindfulness accelerates sukha in formal sitting. I theorize that practicing Joyful Mindfulness got my mind accustomed to ease, humor, and lightness, thus allowing it to connect with sukha more readily during formal practice. That sukha then quietly infuses my daily life and makes daily experiences a bit more joyful, thereby increasing the frequency and intensity of joyful experiences that I can use for Joyful Mindfulness practice. And thus, another happy, virtuous cycle is formed. Joyful Mindfulness works great by itself, but it becomes very powerful in combination with formal mindfulness practice.

Mastering Both Focused and Open Attention

There are two complementary qualities of physical fitness: strength and stamina. To be a well-rounded athlete, it is good to have both. Similarly, there are two complementary qualities of attention: focused attention and open attention. To be an accomplished meditator, it is good to be strong in both.

Focused attention is an intense focus on a chosen object. It is stable, strong, and unwavering. It is like sunlight focused with a lens shining intensely on a single point. It is like a solid piece of rock, majestically unmoved by the distraction of the wind. It is a mind like a closely guarded royal palace where only the most honored guests are allowed to enter and all others are courteously but firmly turned away.

Open attention is a quality of attention willing to meet any object that arrives at the mind or the senses. It is open, flexible, and inviting. It is like ambient sunlight, lending itself to anything and everything. It is like grass, always swaying gently in the wind. It is like water, willing to take on any shape at any time. It is a mind like an open house with a friendly host, where anybody who walks in is welcomed as an honored guest.

The good news is when you are doing mindfulness meditation, you are training both focused attention and open attention at the same time. (Two for the price of one!) That is because mindfulness meditation includes both components. There is the element of moment-to-moment attention that you keep bringing back, which trains focused attention. There is also the element of non-judging and letting go, which trains open attention. Hence, if you only do mindfulness meditation, you will be just fine.

Having said that, however, we found it very useful for our participants to experience the difference between them and to acquire the tools to emphasize training of one or the other if they so choose. The exercise we created is similar to circuit training that some athletes use. Circuit training is a combination of high-intensity cardio and resistance training in the same session. One common way to do it is for trainees to run around a track (cardio) and then stop to do push-ups (resistance), and then run around the track again, and then stop to do sit-ups (resistance), and so on. Trainees alternate between cardio and resistance training, hence developing both strength and stamina at the same time.

In the same way, our circuit training starts with a focused attention exercise for three minutes, and then we go to an open attention exercise for three minutes, and so on. We usually do this for twelve minutes, plus two minutes each of resting the mind on the breath at the beginning and at the end. Here are the instructions we use.

MEDITATION CIRCUIT TRAINING

Let us begin by sitting comfortably in a position that enables you to be both relaxed and alert at the same time, whatever that means to you.

Let us rest the mind. If you like, you can visualize the breath to be a resting place, or a cushion, or a mattress, and let the mind rest on it.

(Short pause)

Let us shift into focused attention. Bring your attention to your breath, or any other object of meditation you choose. Let this attention be stable like a rock, undisturbed by any distraction. If the mind is distracted, gently but firmly bring the mind back. Let's continue this exercise for the remainder of 3 minutes.

(Long pause)

Now we shift into open attention. Bring your attention to whatever you experience and whatever comes to mind. Let this attention be flexible like grass moving in the wind. In this mind, there is no such thing as a distraction. Every object you experience is an object of meditation. Everything is fair game. Let us continue this exercise for the remainder of 3 minutes.

(Long pause)

(Shift to focused attention for 3 minutes. Then shift to open attention for 3 minutes.)

Let us end this sitting by resting the mind. If you like, you can again visualize the breath to be a resting place, or a cushion, or a mattress, and let the mind rest on it.

(Long pause)

Thank you for your attention.

There are a few important features common to both focused and open attention. These features are also common with the original mindfulness meditation we practiced earlier.

The first feature is strong meta-attention (attention of attention). This is because in either meditation, you maintain clear awareness of the movement (or non-movement) of your attention. Hence with enough practice, meta-attention can be strong whether in moving mind (open attention) or still mind (focused attention). The second feature, closely related to the first one, is clarity and vividness of attention. In either meditation, attention can be maintained at high clarity. The analogy is a good torchlight, which can be equally bright whether you shine it at one spot or move it around the room.

The third feature is both meditations require a balance of effort and relaxation. In either case, too much effort makes it tiring and unsustainable, while too little effort causes you to lose your grip on your attention. The classical analogy for this balance is having just the right tension on the strings of a sitar. If the strings are too tight, they break easily, but if they are too loose, they cannot produce beautiful notes. So the strings need to be in the "Goldilocks zone" of being not too tight and not too loose.

I suggest one fun way of maintaining this balance is to play it like a video game. When playing a game on the Xbox, it is most fun when the difficulty setting makes the game just difficult enough to be challenging but not so difficult that you will lose every time. So I like to start a game at a beginner setting and increase the difficulty as I get better at it. We can play the same way in meditation, especially because we get to control the difficulty setting. Initially, we can make the game easy. For example, we can tell ourselves, "If I can sit for just five minutes, and I can maintain a solid attention on my breath for ten continuous breaths anytime during these five minutes, I win!" If you can beat the game at this difficulty setting, say, 90 percent of the time, you can increase the difficulty setting for more fun. Once again, the key is to create just enough difficulty to be challenging, but not enough to discourage you. One funny thing I discovered about playing this game is after I became quite good at it, the lowest difficulty setting became really fun. That setting for me is, "Just rest my mind for ten minutes, in an alert sort of way." That's it, just rest. I like it so much that I still play at this setting a lot in between days when I play the more challenging games. It is a game in which the easiest setting never gets boring.

"I got you this book on mindfulness meditation instead of an Xbox. It's just as fun!"

The final feature, closely related to the third feature, is that in either meditation it is possible to get into a very good state of ease and flow. When you are engaged in an activity you are very good at, such as skiing, dancing, or writing code, and if you are in a state where your full attention is on the activity and it is fun, easy, and sufficiently challenging at the same time, then you may get into a state of flow in which you are performing at your best yet your mind is at ease. Similarly, with enough practice, it is possible to become skillful at playing with attention and getting into a state of flow when it feels fun and easy at the same time, just by sitting. Very cool.

Zen and a Walking Baby

One of the best analogies I have ever come across for meditation practice is a baby learning to walk.

I remember my daughter taking her first step when she was about nine months old. One beautiful step. One step was all she could manage before she would fall, in the über-cute way that only babies can fall. (Everybody say, "Awwwww.") Eventually, she graduated from one step to two steps. And then she plateaued for a while. For a couple of months, she could walk no more than one or two steps before she would fall. (Awwwww.) Then a few days after her first birthday, I noticed her walking four steps. That same day, she doubled that achievement and maxed out at eight steps. (Yes, I measured—I'm an engineer.) The next day, she seemed to plateau at eight steps, but in the late afternoon, she managed sixteen steps before she fell. In the evening, she exceeded thirty steps. Once she broke that barrier, she could walk. On that day, she mastered walking. (Awwwww.)

I found an important similarity between that experience and my own meditation practice. There seem to be two stages in one's meditation progress. I call the two stages "initial access" and "consolidation." The initial access stage is when you find yourself able to access a certain state of mind, but you cannot maintain that mind for very long. For example, you may serendipitously find yourself in a state of mind where you are very calm and alert, and feel a deep sense of joy permeating your mind, but after just a few minutes, you lose it. This stage is like a baby taking her very first step. The baby is finally able to access the experience of walking. She finally knows what it feels like, but it only lasts a single step, maybe two, and then it is over.

The consolidation stage is the long process of going from walking one step to being able to walk around the house. For a meditator, it is becoming able to bring up a state of mind on demand, at a desired intensity and duration. Progress in this stage seems to be an exponential function that looks like a hockey stick on a graph, which means that you go for a frustratingly long time seemingly without any meaningful progress, and then suddenly—*boom*—within a very short period, you make huge progress and arrive at full consolidation. It's like my daughter plateauing at two steps for months and then suddenly, in the space of two days, becoming able to walk. To the casual observer, it may look like she learned to walk in just two days, but in reality, she did it over three months. It is her constant practice over three months that enabled the last two days of sudden progress and mastery.

I think the lesson to be learned is to avoid feeling discouraged when your meditation does not seem to be progressing. If you understand the process, you may understand that when change does come, it will come suddenly, and every moment of effort brings you a little closer to that point. The classical analogy is ice breaking up on a frozen lake. To a casual observer, the breakup seems like a sudden phenomenon, but it is actually due to a long period of gradual melting of the underlying ice structure. In Zen, we call it gradual effort and sudden enlightenment.

So the next time you see a baby learn to walk, pay some attention. That baby is really a Zen master teaching you a thing or two about progress in your meditation. (Everybody say, "Awwwww.")

"She's very advanced."

CHAPTER FOUR

All-Natural, Organic Self-Confidence

Self-Awareness That Leads to Self-Confidence

You cannot solve a problem with the same mind that created it.

—Albert Einstein

Once upon a time in ancient India, a thief running away from guards noticed a beggar sleeping in a dark alley. He secretly put the small but priceless piece of jewelry he had just stolen into the pocket of the beggar. He then ran away, intending to come back and steal from the beggar after he outran the guards. Overnight, the thief was accidentally killed during a struggle with the guards. The beggar was now a rich man. In his pocket, he had enough wealth to live comfortably for life, but he never once checked his own pocket, so he never knew. He lived the rest of his life as a beggar.

You never know what you will find when you look within—there may be hidden treasures.

Clarity

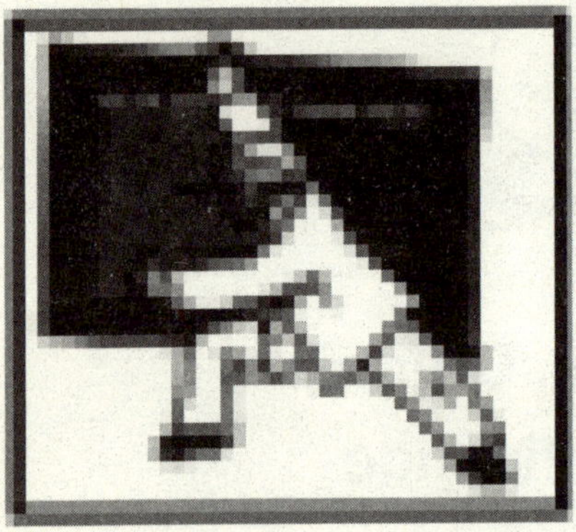

This chapter is about looking within ourselves. If the whole chapter can be encapsulated in a single word, that word is *clarity.* Deepening self-awareness is about developing clarity within oneself. There are two specific qualities we like to develop—resolution and vividness—as illustrated by the pictures above.

The picture on the right is different from the picture on the left in two ways. First, the resolution is higher, so we can see a lot more details. Second, there is more brightness and contrast, so we can see the image more vividly. The combination of resolution and vividness makes the image more useful to us. In the same way, the practices in this chapter will help us perceive our emotions more clearly in two ways. Firstly, we can increase the resolution (or precision) at which we perceive our emotions, so we can see emotions the moments they arise and cease, and subtle changes in between. Secondly, we increase their brightness and contrast so we can see them more vividly than before. This combination will give us very useful high-fidelity information about our emotional life.

About Self-Awareness

Daniel Goleman defines self-awareness as "knowing one's internal states, preferences, resources and intuitions."[1] I like this description because it suggests that self-awareness goes beyond insight into one's moment-to-moment emotional experience; it expands into a broader domain of "self," such as understanding our own strengths and weaknesses and being able to access our own inner wisdom.

Self-awareness is the key domain of emotional intelligence that enables all the others. This is because self-awareness engages the neocortex (the thinking brain) in the process of emotion. Self-awareness maps onto areas of the thinking brain that have to do with self-focused attention and language, so when we are engaged in strong self-awareness, those areas of the brain light up, and that can mean the difference between screaming at some guy or being able to stop and tell yourself, "I cannot scream at that guy; he is the CEO!" Our engagement of the neocortex in every experience of emotion is a necessary step in gaining control over our emotional lives. Mingyur Rinpoche has a poetic metaphor for describing it, he says the moment you can see a raging river, it means you are already rising above it. Similarly, the moment you can see an emotion, you are no longer fully engulfed in it.

Self-Awareness Competencies

Daniel Goleman defines the concept of *emotional competence* as "a learned capability based on emotional intelligence that results in outstanding performance at work."[2] He suggests that there are three emotional competencies under the domain of self-awareness:

1. Emotional awareness: Recognizing one's emotions and their effects
2. Accurate self-assessment: Knowing one's strengths and limits
3. Self-confidence: A strong sense of one's self-worth and capabilities

The key difference between emotional awareness and accurate self-assessment is that the former operates mostly at the level of physiology and the latter operates mostly at the level of meaning. Emotional awareness is my accurately perceiving emotions in my body, knowing where they come from, and understanding how they affect my behavior. Accurate self-assessment, in contrast, goes beyond the emotions I feel and includes knowledge into myself as a human being. It asks questions like: What are my strengths and weaknesses? What are my resources and limitations? What matters to me? Accurate self-assessment builds on emotional awareness.

Each of these three competencies is very useful at work and in life. We discussed in Chapter 1 how a strong emotional awareness, particularly in the body, enhances our access to our intuition. Emotional awareness also has direct implications on our self-motivation. We can best motivate ourselves by aligning what we do with our innermost values, and strong emotional awareness gives us conscious access to those values. We will explore this in more detail in Chapter 6 when we look into motivation.

Emotional awareness may even have a direct impact on the bottom line. For example, organizational psychologists Dr. Cary Cherniss and Dr. Robert Caplan reported that teaching emotional awareness skills to financial advisors at American Express Financial Advisors resulted in more revenue per advisor.[3] Those financial advisors learned to identify their own emotional reactions in challenging situations and became more aware of unproductive self-talk that led to self-doubt and shame. Having that emotional awareness enabled them to employ coping strategies that eventually resulted in them becoming more effective at their work, earning more money for themselves, and presumably giving clients better financial advice. (Related: I taught my own financial advisor mindfulness meditation, and he thought I was just being nice.)

Accurate self-assessment is also referred to as "self-objectivity." It is useful for everyone, but especially useful for managers. Quoting Daniel Goleman:

> *Among several hundred managers from twelve different organizations, Accurate Self-Assessment was the hallmark of superior performance. . . . Individuals with the Accurate Self-Assessment competence are aware of their abilities and limitations, seek out feedback and learn from their mistakes, and know where they need to improve and when to work with others who have complementary strengths. Accurate Self-Assessment was the competence found in virtually every "star performer" in a study of several hundred knowledge workers—computer scientists, auditors and the like—at companies such as AT&T and 3M. . . . On 360-degree competence assessments, average performers typically overestimate their strengths, whereas star performers rarely do; if anything, the stars tended to underestimate their abilities, an indicator of high internal standards.*[4]

Essentially, none of us is perfect, and accurate self-assessment helps us become successful despite our limitations.

Self-confidence is a powerful competency. Norman Fischer has a lovely description of true self-confidence:

> *Self-confidence isn't egotism. . . . When you are truly self-confident, you are flexible with regard to ego: you can pick up ego when necessary, but you can also put it down when necessary in order to learn something completely new through listening. And if you find that you can't put ego down, at least you know that this is so. You can admit it to yourself. It takes profound self-confidence to be humble enough to recognize your own limitations without self-blame.*[5]

Now that we have walked through a couple of chapters together, we have become almost like old friends, so it is time I share a dirty little secret with you: I am actually a very shy person. In fact, when I was growing up, I was shy and socially awkward, befitting the stereotype of the geeky kid who everybody predicted would grow up to be a successful engineer. Today, as an adult, even though I am still very shy, I find myself able to project a quiet but unmistakable self-confidence, whether I am meeting world leaders like Barack Obama, speaking to a large audience, or dealing with a traffic police officer. I watched the video of myself speaking at the United Nations, and I was amazed how confident I appeared. Heck, if I didn't already know the guy on that video, I would have thought him to be very cool.

I am able to project that confidence not because I make the effort to look confident, but because I have a sense of humor about my ego, or my own sense of self-importance. In most situations, when interacting with people, I let my ego become small, humble, and mostly irrelevant, while focusing on bringing kindness and benefit to whomever I am interacting with. At the same time, I let my ego grow to whatever size that allows me to be unintimidated by whomever I am interacting with, whether it is Bill Clinton, Natalie Portman, a traffic cop, or a large audience watching me on YouTube. In that sense, I think of self-confidence as the ability to be as big as Mount Fuji and as small as an insignificant grain of sand at the same time. I let my ego be simultaneously big and small, and I quietly laugh at its absurdity. That is a shy engineer's secret to self-confidence.

Unsurprisingly, self-confidence also turns out to be very useful for work. There are many studies showing the importance of self-confidence in outstanding work performance. For example, one study by a well-known expert in emotional intelligence, Dr. Richard Boyatzis, shows self-confidence to be a distinguishing factor separating the best managers from the merely average ones.[6] In fact, a large meta-analysis of 114 studies shows self-efficacy (a form of self-confidence) to correlate positively with work performance and suggests it may be even more effective than strategies like goal setting, which are widely known to improve work performance.[7]

From Emotional Awareness to Self-Confidence

An easy way to get an injection of self-confidence is to attend a motivational speech where some guy speaking perfect English without my funny accent shouts at you and tells you how great you are, "You can succeed! You are great! You can do it!" And everybody claps. And we all go home feeling great about ourselves, for three days, maybe. In my experience, however, the only highly sustainable source of self-confidence comes from deep self-knowledge and blatant self-honesty.

In my engineer's mind, I think of it as understanding two important modes I operate in: my failure mode and my recovery mode. If I can understand a system so thoroughly I know exactly how it fails, I will also know when it will not fail. I can then have strong confidence in the system, despite knowing it is not perfect, because I know what to adjust for in each situation.

In addition, if I also know exactly how the system recovers after failure, I can be confident even when it fails because I know the conditions in which the system can come back quickly enough that the failure becomes inconsequential. Similarly, by understanding those things about my mind, my emotions, and my capability, I can gain confidence in myself despite my numerous failings and despite looking like I do.

I had an opportunity to put this to the test when I recently spoke at the World Peace Festival in Berlin. I was especially nervous about being on a closing plenary panel because all the other participants were ten times cooler than I was. They were a Nobel peace laureate, a government minister, a renowned philanthropist, and my friend Deepak Chopra, while I was just some guy from Google. I felt like a kid sitting at the adults' table. Worse, I usually had to spend a lot of time preparing for public speaking because it took me conscious mental processing to properly articulate English words. It was challenging for me to be speaking and thinking at the same time. On this occasion, I had no idea what the panel moderator would ask me until literally one minute before the event began, so I could not adequately prepare.

Happily, my mindfulness training kicked in. First, I remembered to treat my ego with humor and let it be small enough that my "self" did not matter, but big enough that I felt perfectly comfortable speaking alongside a Nobel peace laureate at a peace conference as an equal. Then I remembered my strengths and limitations—for example, I knew I was an expert at wisdom practices in a corporate setting but knew nothing about creating national peace infrastructures, so I focused on adding value where I could contribute the most. I also reminded myself that my main strength was my ability to contribute to an atmosphere of peace and humor in a room, so I stayed in a meditative state of Joyful Mindfulness (see Chapter 3) as much as I could. Finally, I understood my most immediate failure mode, which was stumbling on English words while speaking, and my recovery mode strategy, which was to breathe deeply, smile, maintain mindfulness, and not let my occasional faltering bother me. Employing all these self-awareness–based strategies, I was able to maintain my confidence the entire time. I am glad I learned this stuff.

The type of deep self-knowledge and blatant self-honesty needed for sustainable self-confidence means having nothing to hide from oneself. It comes from accurate self-assessment. If we can assess ourselves accurately, we can clearly and objectively see our greatest strengths *and* our biggest weaknesses. We become honest to ourselves about our most sacred aspirations and darkest desires. We learn about our deepest priorities in life, what is important to us, and what is not important that we can let go. Eventually, we reach a point where we are comfortable in our own skins. There are no skeletons in our closets we do not already know about. There is nothing about ourselves we cannot deal with. This is the basis of self-confidence.

Accurate self-assessment, in turn, comes from strong emotional awareness. I think of it as receiving emotional data at a very high signal-to-noise ratio (that is, getting a clean signal). To strengthen our emotional awareness, we must carefully study our emotional experience. We are like a trainer studying a horse; the more we carefully observe the horse in different situations, the more we understand its tendencies and behaviors, and the more skillfully we can work with it. With that clarity, we create a space that allows us to view our own emotional lives as if seeing it as an objective third party. In other words, we gain objectivity, and we begin to perceive each emotional experience clearly and objectively as it is. This is the clean signal that creates the conditions for accurate self-assessment.

This suggests a simple linear relationship between the three emotional competencies of self-awareness—that strong emotional awareness leads to more accurate self-assessment, which in turn leads to higher self-confidence.

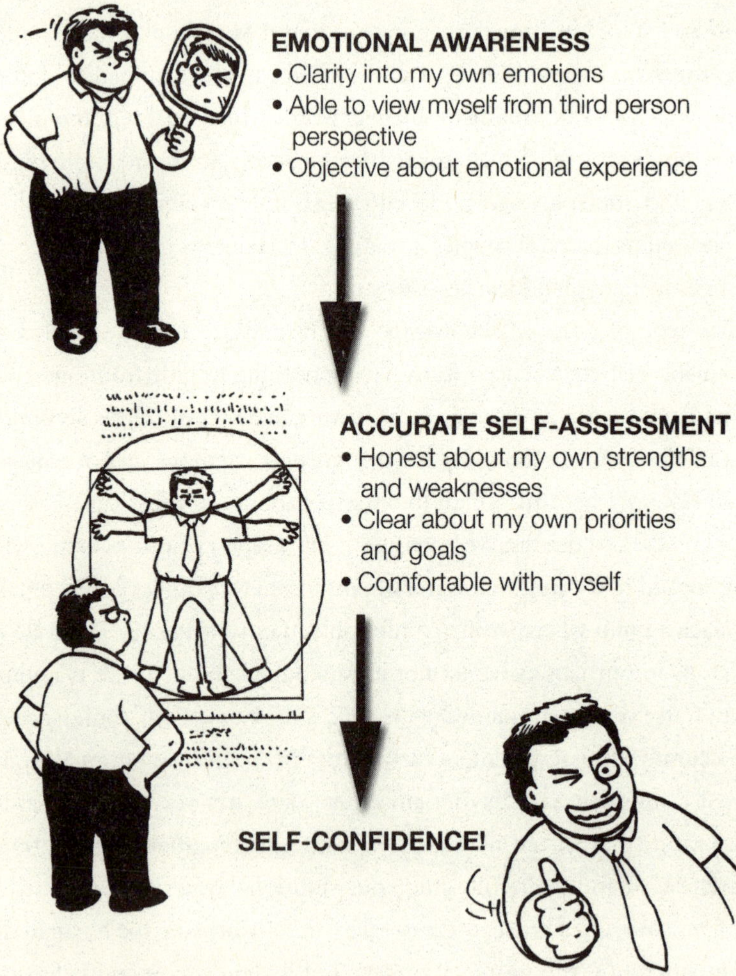

Developing Self-Awareness

Some things in life are so glaringly obvious, they are hidden in plain sight. An example is the similarity between self-awareness and mindfulness. Compare, for example, the definitions of each by two giants in their respective fields:

> *Self-awareness . . . is a neutral mode that maintains self-reflectiveness even in the midst of turbulent emotions.*
>
> —Daniel Goleman[8]

> *Mindfulness means paying attention in a particular way: on purpose, in the present moment, and non-judgmentally.*
>
> —Jon Kabat-Zinn[9]

They are essentially talking about the same thing! Self-awareness (as defined by Dan) is mindfulness (as defined by Jon). This was actually the key insight that led me to develop Search Inside Yourself. Being a practitioner myself, I already knew that mindfulness is trainable, and if self-awareness is essentially mindfulness, then self-awareness must also be trainable in similar ways. Eureka! It was this insight and following that line of inquiry that led my team and me to develop an entire curriculum for emotional intelligence.

The traditional analogy of this mind is a fluttering flag on a flagpole. The flag represents the mind. In the presence of strong emotions, the mind may be turbulent like a flag fluttering violently in the wind. The flagpole represents mindfulness—it keeps the mind steady and grounded despite all that emotional movement. This stability is what allows us to view ourselves with third-person objectivity.

Talking about the flag and the mind reminds me of a Zen joke. A large group of people gathered to listen to a talk by a Zen teacher. One guy in the audience got distracted by a fluttering flag and said, "Flag is moving." Another guy said, "No, wind is moving." The third guy, the wisest person in the audience said, "No, my friends, mind is moving." A fourth guy, getting really annoyed, said, "Mouths are moving."

Generic, plain vanilla mindfulness meditation alone can help you develop self-awareness. We feel, however, that formal practices can work even better, so we introduced two formal practices in our class, both based on mindfulness. The first one, Body Scan, functions at the level of physiology and works best for developing emotional awareness. The second, Journaling, functions at the level of meaning and works best for developing accurate self-assessment.

These two practices, by facilitating self-knowledge and self-honesty, also create the conditions for self-confidence.

Body Scan

In Chapter 1, we mentioned that emotion is a physiological experience, therefore the best way to create a high-resolution awareness of emotion is by applying mindfulness to the body. The simplest way to do it is to bring mindfulness to your body all the time. Every time you bring mindful attention to your body, you create conditions for neurological changes that allow you to become even more perceptive of your body, and consequently, of the process of emotion.

For those of you who like to do things systemically, there is a formal practice called body scan. It is one of the core practices in Jon Kabat-Zinn's highly successful Mindfulness-Based Stress Reduction (MBSR) course. The practice itself is very simple: we just systematically bring moment-to-moment non-judging attention to different parts of our bodies, starting from the top of our head and moving down to the tips of our toes (or vice versa), noticing all sensation or lack of sensation. Remember that the important thing is attention, not sensation. Hence, it does not matter if you experience sensation or not, it only matters that you pay attention.

In MBSR, depending on the teacher, this practice can last for twenty to forty-five minutes. In Search Inside Yourself, the practice is shorter, concentrating only on parts of the body most involved in the experience of emotion. In addition, because Search Inside Yourself is primarily an emotional intelligence course, we also invite participants to experience their physiological correlates of emotion during the second half of the sitting.

BODY SCAN

Settling Attention

Let us begin by sitting comfortably for 2 minutes. Sit in a position that enables you to be both relaxed and alert at the same time, whatever that means to you.

(continued)

Now, let us breathe naturally and bring very gentle attention to the breath. You can either bring attention to the nostrils, the abdomen, or the entire body of breath, whatever that means to you. Become aware of in breath, out breath, and space in between.

Scan Body

Head

Now bring your attention to the top of your head, ears, and back of your head. Notice sensations, or lack of sensations, for 1 minute.

Face

Now move your attention to your face. Your forehead, eyes, cheeks, nose, lips, mouth, and inside of your mouth (gums, tongue) for 1 minute.

Neck and Shoulders

Move your attention to your neck, the inside of your throat, and your shoulders for 1 minute.

Back

Move your attention to your lower back, mid back, and upper back for 1 minute. The back carries a lot of our load and stores a lot of our tension. So let us give our backs the kind and loving attention they deserve.

Front

Now move your attention to the chest and stomach for 1 minute. If it is possible for you, try to bring attention to your internal organs, whatever that means to you.

Entire Body at Once

And now, bring your attention to your entire body all at once for 1 minute.

Scan for Emotion

Did you find any emotion in your body? If there is any, just notice its presence in the body. If not, just notice the absence of emotions, and catch one if it arises in the next 2 minutes.

Positive Emotion

Let us now try to experience a positive emotion in the body.

Bring to mind a memory of a happy, joyous event or a time when you were optimal and productive or a time when you felt confident.

Experience the feeling of positive emotion. Now, bring your attention to your body. What does that positive emotion feel like in the body? In the face? Neck, chest, back? How are you breathing? Any difference in level of tension? Let us just experience it for 3 minutes.

Returning to Grounding

Let us now return to the present. If you find an emotionally charged thought, just let it go.

Bring your attention to either your body or your breath, whichever your mind finds more stability in. And let's just settle the mind there for 2 minutes.

(Long pause)

Thank you for your attention.

Notice that we only invite you to bring up a positive emotion in this exercise, not a negative one. We wait until the next chapter to do an exercise involving negative emotions because that is when we introduce tools for dealing with them. In class, we also do not want to ask our participants to bring up negative emotions without first introducing tools to manage them because doing so would upset our lawyers, and we like our lawyers.

I want to encourage everyone to try out the formal body scanning practice because it has many important benefits. First, it works better than just merely bringing mindfulness to day-to-day activities. The main reason is focus. When you are doing normal activities, you can likely only dedicate a small percentage of your attention to your body, unless you have a highly trained mind, like Thich Nhat Hanh does, or your activity involves devoting full attention to your body, as in competitive dancing, or you are Thich Nhat Hanh engaged in competitive dancing. In contrast, if you are doing nothing else but formal body scanning, you can focus far more of your attention to your body, and attention is what drives neurological change.

One of the participants in our Search Inside Yourself class is a manager called Jim. After a few weeks of practicing body scan, he told me, "I realized that I suppressed emotions into my body. That made me experience physical disablement that would frequently cause me to miss work. This practice has helped me come to work more frequently." Jim has nine direct reports, so his practice benefited at least ten people at work. ("Jim" is not his real name, but I assure you he has a real body.)

"Scan your own body!"

A second benefit of body scan is it helps you sleep. I know that because in MBSR, participants practice body scan lying down, and in every class, at least one person ends up snoring (with everyone else thinking, "Stop snoring. I'm trying to meditate, damn it!"). I am not entirely sure why body scan is so conducive to sleep, but from my own experience, I can think of a few reasons. By bringing attention to the body, we are helping it relax. Very often, bodily tension builds up because we are not paying attention to the body, so the mere presence of attention corrects that problem. Also, body scan and other gentle, mindfulness-based exercises bring the mind to rest. So body scan relaxes both the body and the mind, and if you do it lying down, it is easy to fall asleep. If you have problems sleeping, this might help you.

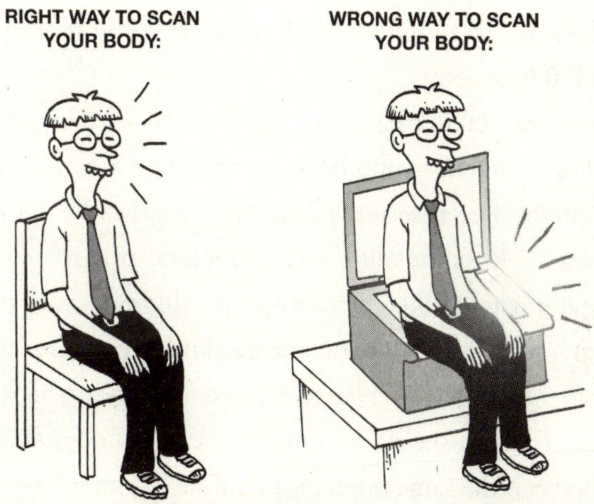

Journaling

Journaling is the practice of self-discovery by writing to yourself. It is an important exercise to help you discover what is in your mind that is not in a clear, conscious view. Usually, when we write, we are trying to communicate a thought with another person. This exercise is different. You're not trying to communicate with somebody else. Instead, you are trying to let your thoughts flow onto paper so you can see what comes up.

The exercise itself is very simple. You give yourself a certain amount of time, say, three minutes, and you are given (or you give yourself) a prompt, which for our purposes is an open-ended sentence such as "What I am feeling now is . . ." For those three minutes, write down whatever comes to mind. You may write about the prompt, or you may write about anything else that comes to mind. Try not to think about what you're going to write—just write. It does not matter how closely you follow the prompt; just let all your thoughts flow onto the paper. There is only one rule: do not stop writing until your time is up. If you run out of things to write, just write, *I ran out of things to write. I have nothing to write. I still have nothing to write. . . .* until you have something to write about again. Remember, you are writing to yourself, for yourself, and you will never have to show this to another person unless you want to. Hence, you can do this with full honesty.

You can think of journaling as mindfulness of thoughts and emotions; paying moment-to-moment, non-judging attention to thoughts and emotions as they arise; and facilitating their flow by putting them on paper. There are a couple other ways of looking at it. My engineer's way of looking at it is an unfiltered brain dump—dumping your mind-stream onto paper. A more poetic way of looking at it is seeing your thoughts as a gently flowing stream and trying to capture that flow on paper.

This practice is so simple, you may wonder if it does anything useful at all. I wondered the same thing the first time Norman Fischer explained it to me, but the research blew my mind. A study by Stefanie Spera, Eric Buhrfeind, and James Pennebaker had a group of laid-off professionals write to themselves about their feelings for five consecutive days for twenty minutes each day.[10] These people found new jobs at a much higher rate than the people in the non-writing control group. After eight months, 68.4 percent of them found jobs, versus 27.3 percent from the control group. Those numbers just blew my mind. Usually, if an intervention can make a difference of a few percentage points, you can publish a paper. But here, we are not talking about 3 percentage points. We are talking about more than 40 percentage points! And all it took was one hundred minutes of intervention. Oh, wow.

How much journaling do you have to do before you experience a measurable change? Quoting an article that appeared on March 2, 2009, on the *Very Short List (VSL): Science* website:[11]

> *Twenty years ago, University of Texas psychologist James Pennebaker concluded that students who wrote about their most meaningful personal experiences for 15 minutes a day several days in a row felt better, had healthier blood work, and got higher grades in school. But a new study from the University of Missouri shows that a few minutes of writing will also suffice.*
>
> *Researchers asked 49 college students to take two minutes on two consecutive days and write about something they found to be emotionally significant. The participants registered immediate improvements in mood and performed better on standardized measures of physiological well-being. An extended inward look isn't necessary, the study concludes; merely "broaching the topic on one day and briefly exploring it the next" is enough to put things in perspective.*

Four minutes can make a measurable difference. That exploding sound is the sound of my mind being blown.

One fun way of having a daily journaling practice is to write a different prompt on each piece of paper, put them all in a fishbowl (a dry one, I recommend), then pick out one or two at random each day. Here are some suggested prompts:

- What I am feeling now is . . .
- I am aware that . . .
- What motivates me is . . .
- I am inspired by . . .
- Today, I aspire to . . .
- What hurts me is . . .
- I wish . . .
- Others are . . .
- I made a happy mistake . . .
- Love is . . .

Here are instructions for the accurate self-assessment exercise. Notice that in addition to the usual journaling, we also added a primer to open your mind into a frame conducive to this exercise.

JOURNALING FOR SELF-ASSESSMENT

Prime

Before we begin journaling, let's prime the mind.

Let's spend 2 minutes thinking about one or more instances in which you responded positively to a challenging situation and the outcome was very satisfying to you. You felt you did great. If you are considering more than one instance, think about whether any connections or patterns are emerging.

Now, let's take a moment to relax mentally.

(30-second pause)

Journal

Prompts (2 minutes per prompt):

- Things that give me pleasure are . . .
- My strengths are . . .

Prime

Now let's spend 2 minutes thinking about one or more instances in which you responded negatively to a challenging situation and the outcome was very unsatisfying to you. You felt that you performed badly, and you wish there were something you could change. If you are considering more than one instance, think about whether any connections or patterns are emerging.

Now, let's take a moment to relax mentally.

(30-second pause)

Journal

Prompts (2 minutes per prompt):

- Things that annoy me are . . .
- My weaknesses are . . .

Take a few minutes to read what you wrote to yourself.

My Emotions Are Not Me

As we deepen our self-awareness, we eventually arrive at a very important key insight: we are not our emotions.

We usually think of our emotions as being us. This is reflected in the language we use to describe them. For example, we say, "I am angry" or "I am happy" or "I am sad," as if anger, happiness, or sadness are us, or become who we are. To the mind, our emotions become our very existence.

With enough mindfulness practice, you may eventually notice a subtle but important shift—you may begin to feel that emotions are simply what you feel, not who you are. Emotions go from being existential ("I am") to experiential ("I feel"). With even more mindfulness practice, there may be another subtle but important shift—you may begin to see emotions simply as physiological phenomena. Emotions become what we experience in the body, so we go from "I am angry" to "I experience anger in my body."

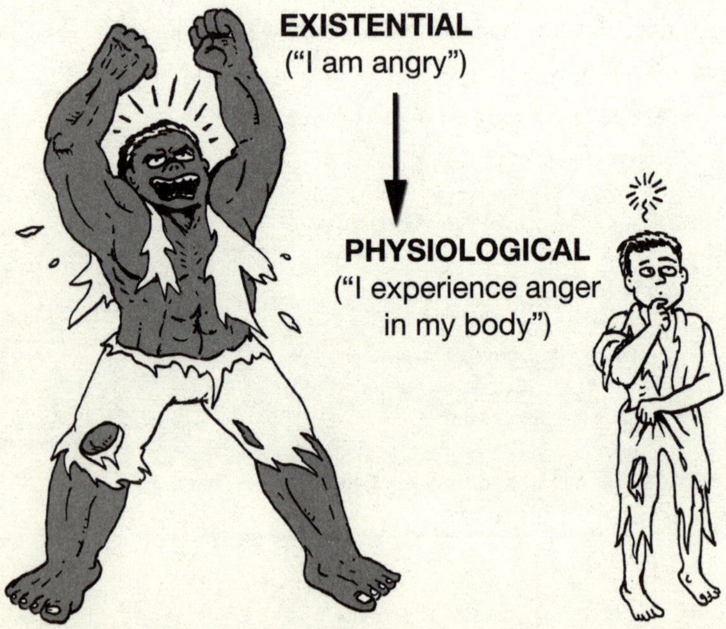

This subtle shift is extremely important because it suggests the possibility of mastery over our emotions. If my emotions are who I am, then there is very little I can do about it. However, if emotions are simply what I experience in my body, then feeling angry becomes a lot like feeling pain in my shoulders after an extreme workout; both are just physiological experiences over which I have influence. I can soothe them. I can ignore them and go get some ice cream, knowing I will feel better in a few hours. I can experience them mindfully. Fundamentally, I can act on them because they are not my core being.

In meditative traditions, we have a beautiful metaphor for this insight. Thoughts and emotions are like clouds—some beautiful, some dark—while our core being is like the sky. Clouds are not the sky; they are phenomena in the sky that come and go. Similarly, thoughts and emotions are not who we are; they are simply phenomena in mind and body that come and go.

Possessing this insight, one creates the possibility of change within oneself.

CHAPTER FIVE

Riding Your Emotions like a Horse

Developing Self-Mastery

One can have no smaller or greater mastery than mastery of oneself.

—Leonardo da Vinci

The theme of this chapter can be summarized in these four words:

From Compulsion to Choice

Once upon a time in ancient China, a man on a horse rode past a man standing on the side of the road. The standing man asked, "Rider, where are you going?" The man on the horse answered, "I don't know. Ask the horse."

This story provides a metaphor for our emotional lives. The horse represents our emotions. We usually feel compelled by our emotions. We feel we have no control over the horse, and we let it take us wherever it wants to. Fortunately, it turns out that we can tame and guide the horse. It begins with understanding the horse and observing its preferences, tendencies, and behaviors. Once we understand the horse, we learn to communicate and work with it skillfully. Eventually, it takes us wherever we want to go. Hence we create choice for ourselves. We can then choose to ride into the sunset and look cool like John Wayne.

The last chapter, when we explored self-awareness, is about understanding the horse. In this chapter, we will make use of self-awareness to gain mastery over our emotions. In other words, we will learn to ride the horse.

About Self-Regulation

When we think of self-regulation, we usually think only of self-control, like the not-screaming-at-the-CEO type of self-control. If that is all you are thinking, my friends, you are missing all the good, yummy stuff. Self-regulation goes far beyond self-control. Daniel Goleman identifies five emotional competencies under the domain of self-regulation:

1. Self-control: Keeping disruptive emotions and impulses in check
2. Trustworthiness: Maintaining standards of honesty and integrity
3. Conscientiousness: Taking responsibility for personal performance
4. Adaptability: Flexibility in handling change
5. Innovation: Being comfortable with novel ideas, approaches, and information

There is one commonality that underlies all these competences: **choice.** Everybody wants to have all these qualities. We all like to be adaptable and innovative, for example. Who among us does not want to maintain our standards of honesty and integrity? Yet, a lot of us do not succeed at upholding these qualities all the time. Why? Because we often feel compelled by our emotions to move in a different direction. If, however, we have the ability to turn compulsion into choice, then all these qualities may become enabled for us, and we may choose to exercise them if we wish.

The ability to move from compulsion to choice is the common enabler for all these competencies.

Self-Regulation Is Not Avoiding or Suppressing Emotions

After teaching Search Inside Yourself for a while, we realized that while it is important to explain what self-regulation is, it is equally important to explain what self-regulation is not. The simple reason is many people think self-regulation is simply about suppressing distressing emotions. Happily, that is not the case.

Self-regulation is not about avoiding emotions. There are situations in which feeling painful emotions is appropriate. For example, when your best friend shares sad news with you, it is probably best if you also share some of her sadness. Also, if you are a doctor giving very bad news to a patient, you probably don't want to avoid feeling bad. You definitely do not want a big grin on your face when you tell your patient he only has one month to live—that would be awkward.

Self-regulation is also not about denying or repressing true feelings. Feelings carry valuable information, so if you deny or repress them, you lose that information. One Search Inside Yourself participant at Google, for example, learned to listen closely to his feelings and began to grasp the full extent of his dissatisfaction in his current role. In response, he moved into another role at Google shortly after the course and became much happier and more effective at his work.

Self-regulation is not about never having certain emotions. It is about becoming very skillful with them. For example, I was told that in Buddhist psychology, there is an important difference between anger and indignation: anger arises out of powerlessness, while indignation arises out of power. Because of that difference, when you feel angry, you feel out of control, but when you feel indignant, you can retain full control of your mind and emotion. Hence, you can be emotional and fighting for change without ever losing your cool. Indignation is, therefore, a skillful state and a good example of self-regulation at its best. I think the person who best personified this was Gandhi. Gandhi was not an angry man, but that did not stop him from fighting injustice or leading massive marches. All that time he was fighting, he never lost his calmness or compassion. That's how I want to be when I grow up.

Like Writing on Water

Still, when there are situations in life where you really need to dampen unwholesome thoughts or emotions, what do you do?

I think the first question to ask is whether it is possible to stop an unwholesome thought or emotion from arising in the first place. Based on my own experience, I think it is impossible. In fact, Paul Ekman, one of the most preeminent psychologists in the world, told me he discussed precisely this topic with the Dalai Lama. They both agree that it is impossible to stop a thought or emotion from arising. That must be the correct answer then, since Paul, the Dalai Lama, and I cannot all be wrong at the same time, right?

However, the Dalai Lama added an important point: while we cannot stop an unwholesome thought or emotion from arising, we have the power to let it go, and the highly trained mind can let it go the moment it arises.

The Buddha has a very beautiful metaphor for this state of mind. He calls it "like writing on water."[1] Whenever an unwholesome thought or emotion arises in an enlightened mind, it is like writing on water; the moment it is written, it disappears.

"My client would like the agreement to be written on water."

Practice of Letting Go

One of the most important life-changing insights gained in meditation is that pain and suffering are qualitatively distinct, and one does not necessarily follow the other. The origin of this insight is the practice of letting go.

Letting go is an extremely important skill. It is one of the essential foundations of meditation practice. As usual, the Zen tradition has the funniest way of articulating this key insight. In the words of Sengcan, the Third Patriarch of Zen, "The Great Way is without difficulty, just cease having preferences."[2] When the mind becomes so free that it is capable of letting go even of preferences, the Great Way is no longer difficult.

The central importance of letting go leads to a very important question: is it possible to let go and still appreciate and fully experience the ups and downs of life? The way I like to ask the question is: can you have your karma and eat cake too?

I think it is possible. The key is to let go of two things: grasping and aversion. Grasping is when the mind desperately holds on to something and refuses to let it go. Aversion is when the mind desperately keeps something away and refuses to let it come. These two qualities are flip sides of each other. Grasping and aversion together account for a huge percentage of the suffering we experience, perhaps 90 percent, maybe even 100 percent.

When we experience any phenomenon, we begin with contact between sense organ and object, then sensation and perception arise, and immediately after, grasping or aversion arises (some meditative traditions classify the mind itself as a sense, thus elegantly extending this model of experience to mental phenomenon as well as physical phenomenon). The key insight here is that grasping and aversion are separate from sensation and perception. They arise so closely together that we do not normally notice the difference.

However, as your mindfulness practice becomes stronger, you may notice the distinction and maybe even the tiny gap between them. For example, after sitting for a long time, you may feel pain in your back, and almost immediately after that, you may feel aversion. You tell yourself, "I hate this pain. I do not want this sensation. Go away!" With enough mindfulness practice, you may notice that both experiences are distinct. There is the experience of physical pain, and there is the separate experience of aversion. The untrained mind lumps them into one indivisible experience, but the trained mind sees two distinct experiences, one leading to the arising of the other.

Once your mind reaches that level of perceptive resolution, two very important opportunities become available to you.

The first important opportunity is the possibility of experiencing pain without suffering. The theory is that aversion, not the pain itself, is the actual cause of suffering; the pain is just a sensation that creates that aversion. Hence, if the mind recognizes this and then becomes able to let go of aversion, then the experience of pain may lead to greatly reduced suffering—perhaps no suffering at all. Jon Kabat-Zinn has a great example of how this theory works in practice. Here, he tells the story of a man in his Mindfulness-Based Stress Reduction (MBSR) clinic:

> *Another man, in his early seventies, came to the clinic with severe pain in his feet. He came to the first class in a wheelchair. . . . That first day he told the class that the pain was so bad he just wanted to cut off his feet. He didn't see what meditating could possibly do for him, but things were so bad that he was willing to give anything a try. Everybody felt incredibly sorry for him. . . . He came to the second class on crutches rather than in the wheelchair. After that he used only a cane. The transition from wheelchair to crutches to cane spoke volumes to us all as we watched him from week to week. He said at the end that the pain hadn't changed much but that his attitude toward his pain had changed a lot.*[3]

One of the most interesting historical figures to have acquired this insight was Roman Emperor Marcus Aurelius, the last of the Five Good Emperors. He wrote:

> *If you are distressed by anything external, the pain is not due to the thing itself, but to your estimate of it; and this you have the power to revoke at any moment.*

Funny enough (in our context), this quote originates from the collection of his writings entitled *Meditations.*

The second important opportunity is the possibility of experiencing pleasure without the aftertaste of unsatisfactoriness. The biggest problem with pleasant experiences is that they all eventually cease. The experience itself causes no suffering, but our clinging on to them and our desperate hoping that they do not go away cause suffering. Thich Nhat Hanh has a very nice way of putting it: wilting flowers do not cause suffering; it is the unrealistic desire that flowers not wilt that causes suffering. Hence, if the mind recognizes this and then becomes able to let go of grasping, the pleasant experiences lead to little or no suffering. We can fully enjoy flowers even though they eventually wilt.

By letting go of grasping and aversion, we can fully adopt the letting-go mind and also fully experience life in its glorious Technicolor detail. In fact, we may be able to experience life more vividly with the letting-go mind because it frees us from the noisy interferences of grasping, aversion, and suffering.

Good karma. Good cake. Yum.

"Okay, you don't have to let *everything* go."

General Principles for Dealing with Distress

Four very helpful general principles for dealing with any distressing emotions are:

1. Know when you are not in pain.
2. Do not feel bad about feeling bad.

3. Do not feed the monsters.

4. Start every thought with kindness and humor.

Know When You Are Not in Pain

When you are not in pain, be aware that you are not in pain. This is a very powerful practice on multiple levels. On one level, it increases happiness. When we are suffering from pain, we always tell ourselves, "I'll be so happy if I am free from this pain," but when we are free from that pain, we forget to enjoy freedom from pain. This practice of constantly noticing the lack of distress encourages us to enjoy the sweetness of that freedom, thereby helping us to be happier.

On another level, I find that even when we are experiencing pain, the pain is not constant, especially emotional pain. The pain waxes and wanes, and there are times (perhaps short intervals of minutes or seconds) when a space opens up and we are free from pain. The practice of noticing the lack of distress helps us abide in that small space when it opens up. This space gives us temporary relief and is the basis from which we launch our recovery and find the strength to face our problems.

Do Not Feel Bad About Feeling Bad

We have the tendency to feel bad about feeling bad. I call it "meta-distress," distress about experiencing distress. This is especially true for sensitive and good-hearted people. We berate ourselves by saying things like, "Hey, if I am such a good person, why am I feeling this much envy?" This is even truer for good people with contemplative practices like meditation. We scold ourselves by saying, "Maybe if I was actually a good meditator, I wouldn't feel this way. Therefore, I must be a hypocrite and a useless piece of [insert context-appropriate noun]."

It is important to recognize that distress is a naturally arising phenomenon—we all experience it from time to time. Even Thich Nhat Hanh, the very symbol of enlightened peace in the world, once got so angry at someone he almost wanted to stand up and slug him.

Also recognize that feeling bad about feeling bad is an act of ego. It's a reflection of our ego's image about itself, and the net result is the creation of new distress for no good reason at all. The antidote is to let the ego go, with good humor whenever possible.

And remember, meta-distress is really bad economics.

Do Not Feed the Monsters

Let's pretend that monsters cause our distress, occupying the mind and wreaking havoc on our emotions. What can we do to stop them? They seem so overwhelmingly powerful, we cannot stop them from arising in the mind, and we seem powerless to make them leave.

Happily, it turns out that our monsters need us to feed them in order to survive. If we do not feed them, they will get hungry, and maybe they will go away. Therein lies the source of our power—we cannot stop monsters from arising or force them to leave, but we have the power to stop feeding them.

Take anger, for example. If you are really angry at somebody and then examine that anger with mindfulness, you may find that the anger is not constant from moment to moment; it is constantly waxing or waning subtly. You may also find your mind constantly feeding the anger by retelling one or more stories to yourself over and over. If you then stop telling the stories, you may find the anger dissipating for the lack of fuel. Anger Monster needs to feed on your angry stories. With no stories to eat, Anger Monster gets hungry and sometimes goes away. By not feeding Anger Monster, you save mental energy and Anger Monster may leave you alone to play elsewhere. Anger Monster knows people are giving away plenty of anger food elsewhere.

Not feeding monsters is very good economics.

"Okay, how about for starters, I just stop feeding you carbs?"

Start Every Thought with Kindness and Humor

In every situation, distressing or otherwise, it is useful to begin each thought with kindness and compassion for oneself and others.

In my experience, the most important quality of kindness is its healing effect. Imagine taking a rough, spiky brush and repeatedly brushing it hard and fast on an area of your skin. Eventually, your skin will become inflamed and painful to the touch. Kindness is the quality of gently ceasing that harmful brushing action. If you do that, eventually, the skin will heal.

I also find it very useful to see the humor in my own failings. Every time I lose my temper or have a greedy or spiteful thought that does not go away for a while, it is like I have fallen off the wagon again. Of course, I can interpret falling off the wagon as a humiliating and embarrassing experience. However, it is much more fun to think of the experience as a scene in an old black-and-white comedy. Guy falls off wagon in the context of fast, playful music, makes a funny face, dusts himself off, and then climbs back up on the wagon in a quick, awkward, and jerky motion. It is all very funny. So every time I fail, it is a comedy.

And since I fail so often, my life is a great comedy.

Neural Model of Emotion Regulation

In the brain, emotional reactivity and regulation look a lot like this:

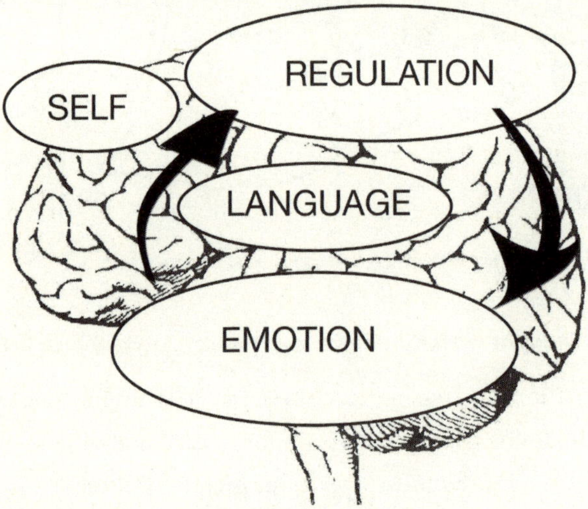

(courtesy of Philippe Goldin)

Stanford research scientist Philippe Goldin explains this process well:

> *In the context of a threat, real or imagined, our emotional state can rapidly shift into fear or anxiety. This shift in emotional reactivity occurs in emotional related brain regions in the limbic system (or the "emotional brain," represented by the "emotion" bubble). A bottom-up signal is sent to other brain regions to recruit from other brain systems to help regulate (the "regulation" bubble) via top-down signals specific aspects of emotional reactivity. When this system is working, the regulatory systems initiate changes in attention, thinking, and*

behavior. Using cognitive perspective taking, we can examine what is the source of the threat and determine what strategies will be most effective in modulating the intensity, duration and interpretation of that ongoing emotion experience. I would also add that especially in human beings, this is likely mediated through our view of self, be it positive or negative or otherwise, and our ability to use language and thinking to modulate and understand our experiences.[4]

This model suggests one way we can think of mindfulness and other practices in this book. Mindfulness helps our thinking brain and our emotional brain communicate more clearly to each other, so they work better together. The engineering types among us can think of mindfulness as increasing the bandwidth of the arrows between the emotion and regulation bubbles so that we get better information flow between them. Mindfulness also gives more power to the thinking brain whenever you need it. You can think of mindfulness as increasing the power output of the regulation systems in the brain so it works even better. In fact, studies suggest it actually does so literally by increasing the neural activity of the executive center of the brain, the medial prefrontal cortex. Finally, mindfulness, in conjunction with other practices and insights in this book, helps us make more skillful use of the self and language bubbles.

Dealing with Triggers

One common situation in which self-regulation skills really come in handy is when we get triggered. That is when a seemingly small situation causes a disproportionally large emotional response in us, such as when our spouse makes an almost innocuous comment about something we do and we just blow up. From an objective, third-party perspective, such an event often seems like making a mountain out of a molehill. For example, all Cindy did was playfully twirl the hair of her husband, John, commenting, "You're getting a little thin up there." John's face immediately became red with anger, and he insulted her with an expletive, right in front of his campaign staff.

The first step in learning to deal with triggers is identifying when you have been triggered. Executive coach Marc Lesser provided these helpful suggestions on things to look out for:

- Body: Shallow breathing, rapid heartbeat, and sick to the stomach
- Emotions: Experiencing a flight-or-flight response, either feeling like a "deer in headlights" or having an emotional outburst (what Goleman famously calls an "amygdala hijack")
- Thoughts: Feeling like a victim, thoughts of blame and judgment, difficulty paying attention

Triggers almost always have long histories behind them. When we get triggered, it is very often because it brings back something from the past, that she's-doing-that-*again* feeling. Triggers are also very often connected to a perceived inadequacy about ourselves that is a source of pain to us, sort of like a raw nerve. For example, if I am feeling very insecure about my performance at work, a mere suggestion from my boss that she is slightly concerned about my project's progress may cause a trigger reaction in me. In contrast, if I am fully confident about my work, my reaction to my boss will be entirely different.

Siberian North Railroad

Here is a practice called the Siberian North Railroad for dealing with triggers. This is a useful practice not only for triggers but also for other situations in which we need to deal with negative or distressing emotions.

The practice has five steps:

1. Stop
2. Breathe

3. Notice

4. Reflect

5. Respond

Jennifer Bevan, one of our class participants, came up with the mnemonic that became the name of the practice. She took the first letter of each step, SBNRR, and created the phrase *SiBerian North RailRoad.* I like the mental imagery behind the mnemonic. It's like you need to cool down from all that heat of an emotional trigger, and where better to cool down than one of the coldest and most remote places in the world?

The first and most important step is to stop. Whenever you feel triggered, just stop. Pausing at the onset of a trigger is a very powerful and important skill. Do not react for just one moment. This moment is known as the **sacred pause.** It enables all the other steps. If you only remember one step in this practice, remember this one. In almost every instance, this one step is enough to make a big difference.

The next step is to breathe. By focusing the mind on the breath, we reinforce the sacred pause. In addition, taking conscious breaths, especially deep ones, calms the body and mind.

After breathing, notice. Experience your emotion by bringing attention to your body. What does this feel like in the body? In the face, neck, shoulder, chest, back? Notice changes in tension and temperature. Apply mindfulness by experiencing it moment-to-moment without judging. What is most important at this point is to try to experience emotional difficulty simply as a physiological phenomenon, not an existential phenomenon. If it is anger you are experiencing, for example, your observation is not "I am angry"; it is "I experience anger in my body."

Now we reflect. Where is the emotion coming from? Is there a history behind it? Is there a self-perceived inadequacy involved? Without judging it to be right or wrong, let's just bring this perspective into the situation. If this experience involves another person, put yourself inside the other person looking out at you. Think about these statements:

- Everybody wants to be happy.
- This person thinks acting this way will make him happy, in some way.

Again, bring perspective without judging it to be right or wrong.

Finally, we respond. Bring to mind ways in which you might respond to this situation that would have a positive outcome. You do not actually have to do it—just imagine the kindest, most positive response. What would that look like?

In our Search Inside Yourself class, before doing the Siberian North Railroad exercise, we invite participants to talk about a situation in which they were triggered. This readies them for the exercise. We usually have them sit in groups of three where each person gets to have a two-minute monologue. The topic of the monologue is:

Describe a situation when you were triggered:

1. What was the event?
2. What were the feelings that arose? What was the very first feeling—anger, retreat?
3. Where in your body did you feel it / do you feel it now?

At home I recommend you think about the last time you were emotionally triggered and ask yourself the questions above. This will prepare you for the following meditation.

SIBERIAN NORTH RAILROAD

Settling Attention

Start with 3 deep breaths.

Bring gentle awareness to the breathing. Bring attention to the in and out breaths, and the spaces in between.

Negative Emotion

Let's now shift gears into a negative emotion for 2 minutes.

Bring to mind a memory of an unhappy event, an experience of frustration, anger, or hurt, or an experience in which you were triggered.

See if you can relive the event and the associated emotions in your mind.

Managing Negative Emotion

Let us now mentally practice our response strategy for 7 minutes.

The first two steps are to stop and breathe. Stopping at the onset of a trigger is the sacred pause. Let us reinforce the pause by focusing the mind on the breath, and not reacting to the emotion. If you want, you may try taking slow, deep breaths. And let's stay in this state of pause for another 30 seconds.

(30-second pause)

The next step is to notice. We notice by experiencing the emotion in the body. Bring your attention to your body. What does an affective emotion feel like in the body? In the face? Neck, shoulders, chest, back? Notice any difference in level of tension or temperature.

Experience it without judging. What is most important at this point is to try to experience emotional difficulty simply as a physiological phenomenon, not an existential phenomenon. For example, the experience is not "I am angry." It is "I experience anger in my body."

Let's take a minute to experience the physiology of emotion in the body.

(60-second pause)

Now we reflect.

Where is the emotion coming from? Is there a history behind it? If this experience involves another person, put yourself inside the other person

(continued)

looking out at you. Think about this statement: "Everybody wants to be happy. This person thinks acting this way will make him happy, in some way." Bring perspective without judging it to be right or wrong.

(30-second pause)

Now we respond.

Bring to mind ways in which you might respond to this situation that would have a positive outcome. You do not actually have to do it—just imagine the kindest, most positive response. What would that look like? Let's spend the next minute or so creating that response.

(60-second pause)

Returning to Grounding

Let us now return to the present for 2 minutes. Bring awareness back to your breath.

(Short pause)

Make a tight fist with your hand, holding any of your residual emotion there. Slowly open your fingers and let go of that energy.

And bring your attention back, either to your body, or your breath, whichever your mind finds more stability in.

And just settle your mind there, for the remainder of 1 minute.

In class, right after the above exercise, we always do Mindful Conversation (see Chapter 3) in pairs to give everyone a chance to process the experience. Those who are comfortable doing so may tell their stories and share their experiences. Those who are not comfortable doing so may just talk about how it felt to go through the process itself.

In this artificial setting, the five-step process takes seven minutes. In real life, the whole process may be over in seconds, which may not give you a lot of time to do it right if you do not have sufficient practice. One way to practice this process is to do it retroactively. That means practicing the reflection and response steps after a triggering event is over. The first three steps (stop, breathe, notice) can be strengthened with sitting mindfulness practice. The last two steps (reflect and respond) are best strengthened with real-life cases. Given how quickly each episode moves, it's hard to train in real time, but it's just as effective to do it "off-line" retroactively. The more time you spend practicing the reflect-and-respond process offline, the better you will be able to do it in the real-life situation.

The next time you are triggered, remember to take the SBNRR.

"Good news, comrades! To help you deal with negative or distressing emotions, the Politburo has come up with a handy mnemonic . . ."

How to Not Strangle Your Mother-In-Law

Derek, one Search Inside Yourself participant who had no prior mindfulness training, told me this story:

My mother-in-law forgot to engage the brake on the stroller with my twenty-month-old daughter inside. The stroller went sailing across the driveway, smacking into one of our cars. Thanks to Search Inside Yourself, instead of coming unglued and saying something stupid, I took two deep breaths and simply refrained from comment. Better still, I did it almost without thinking about it, I just brought attention to my breath at my nostrils, and it just worked. I even recognized the racing in my heart and the sinking, gross feeling in my stomach. It was amazing.

If you ever need examples of people with crazy tempers (me), who usually engage mouth before brain, being able to successfully employ Search Inside Yourself training to not strangle their mothers-in-law, you may tell my story.

Derek did not just refrain from doing something stupid at the moment, but he was also able to later reflect on how sorry his mother-in-law must have felt, and he forgave her carelessness with a few kind words. Last I heard, they lived happily ever after. (Derek's name has been changed to protect him from mothers-in-law.)

Other Ways to Handle Triggers

One way of looking at the Siberian North Railroad approach is as an emotional self-regulation strategy, starting with attentional control and resulting in cognitive change over time. If you understand it that way, it can become a general framework on which we can add other ways of handling triggers. This idea was suggested to me by Philippe Goldin who was, in turn, inspired by a review paper by Kevin Ochsner and James Gross.[5]

As you see below, the timeline begins with the triggering event and goes from left to right. We begin with attentional control but move increasingly toward cognitive change.

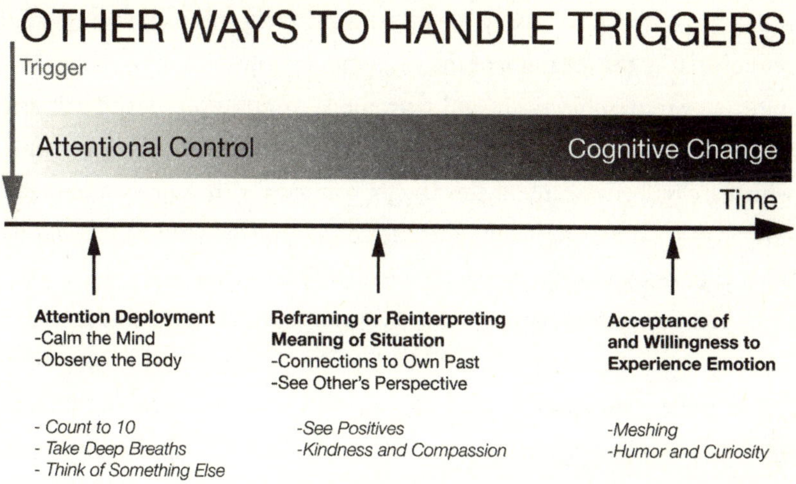

In attentional control, during the moments right after being triggered, we recommend to stop, breathe, and notice, which corresponds to calming the mind and observing the emotional experience in the body. In addition to those, there are other things you can try that may work better for you. One is the standard practice of counting to ten, which is a more deliberate way of invoking the sacred pause. This practice also has the benefit of giving your mind something else to do, thus temporarily distracting it from emotions until it is capable of handling the situation. Another practice is to take slow, deep breaths. Taking deep breaths induces a calming effect, possibly because it stimulates the vagus nerve, which is known to reduce heart rate and blood pressure (I imagine it must be the opposite of the Las Vegas nerve). Lastly, if it gets too overwhelming, you can temporarily distract yourself totally by focusing on something entirely unrelated to the trigger, such as staring at reading materials you have at hand, or perhaps excusing yourself from the room by taking a restroom break ("Break free, go pee").

Attentional control is good and necessary, but often insufficient. Even if your mind is so highly trained that you can let go of the distress and return to calm very quickly, the issues behind the trigger will remain unresolved and you will still be similarly triggered in the future. Hence, cognitive work is also necessary. Cognitive work here means reframing and reinterpreting the meaning of the situation. It almost always involves seeing things more objectively and with more compassion toward self and others. The cognitive practices we recommend are to reflect and respond, which are reflecting on how this trigger connects with your own past and how it must seem from the other person's point of view, and deciding what your optimal response would be if you had a choice.

In addition to these, if it works for you, you can also try seeing positives in this trigger. For example, you just blew up in front of your new boyfriend and are surprised at the level of emotion. This is a perfect time to let things calm down and create space so you can both talk about it, using the situation as an opportunity to help him know you more deeply as a person. Or perhaps this is an opportunity for self-discovery. For example, if you already have a mature meditation practice and something your boss says suddenly makes you feel very vulnerable ("like I'm five years old again"), you have just received valuable education on which aspects of your meditation practice you need to focus. Finally, a more advanced but highly effective practice is to apply kindness and compassion in the situation. This is something we will explore in Chapters 7 and 8.

The final piece of the framework is creating a willingness to experience and accept the emotions—in a way, opening up the heart and mind so they become big enough to effortlessly contain any emotion, like the sky effortlessly containing any cloud. We suggest two practices for this. The first is something Marc Lesser calls "meshing," or visualizing yourself as porous as a mesh screen. As you encounter strong feelings welling up (for example, anger, resentment, fear), let these feelings pass through your body. You can observe these intense feelings moving through you, not sticking to you, and see that they are separate from you. The second, which is my own practice, is to pretend my life is a sitcom and appreciate the humor in every absurd situation. In my life, I have found myself in many unpleasant situations, and most of them can be scenes in a bad comedy, especially bad situations of my own making.

From Self-Regulation to Self-Confidence

Whenever we experience unpleasant emotions, our first instinct is aversion. We do not want these unpleasant feelings; we want them to go away. As a result of this aversion, we shift our thoughts externally toward the other person or environment instead of toward ourselves. For example, when we feel hurt, our thoughts are dominated by how awful the other person is, all because we want to avoid experiencing unpleasant emotions. This process is usually unconscious to most of us.

If, however, through mindfulness and other practices, we bring conscious awareness to this process, then we can see that our externally directed negative thoughts arise mostly from our aversion. Given that insight, if we also develop the capacity to experience our own unpleasant feelings, we may tame aversion, which in turn may tame ruminations and obsessive thoughts. Once we create within ourselves the ability to tame such thoughts, we increase self-confidence.

Earlier in the self-awareness chapter, we talked about how self-confidence can arise from deep understanding of our failure mode and recovery mode. In my engineer's mind, I think of skillfulness in self-regulation as an upgrade to my recovery mechanism. By knowing exactly how a system recovers after failure, I can be confident in it even when it fails because I know the conditions in which the system can come back quickly enough that failure is inconsequential. If, in addition to that, I can upgrade the recovery mechanisms such that it can recover much faster and more cleanly (that is, causing fewer problems), then I can have even more confidence in it and can subject it to even more interesting and challenging environments. We can think of the practices in this chapter as upgrading our recovery mode.

That is how the practices in this chapter can increase our self-confidence.

Jason, a Search Inside Yourself participant, learned to use the insights of self-regulation to improve his own self-confidence. He considered himself a person who gets triggered extremely easily and, consequently, often found himself in socially difficult situations. During Search Inside Yourself, he learned that being triggered can be a "time-limited" experience once he learned to bring attention to his breathing and to stop feeding his monsters. He discovered that all he had to do was calmly experience the unpleasantness by "riding things out" and "letting my body reset" for fifteen to thirty minutes, and then his "view would open up again" and his mind would be clear enough to think properly once more. He also discovered he could gradually shrink the time it takes to "reset" with mindfulness training. Consequently, he gained confidence in himself.

One unintended happy consequence of this was, in his own words, "If I didn't learn all this, I would have quit my job and regretted it." Jason was a skillful engineer, so he was not the only beneficiary of that decision; Google also benefitted by getting to keep him.

Making Friends with Emotions

Ultimately, self-regulation is about making friends with our emotions. All the practices and techniques mentioned in this chapter—the Siberian North Railroad, not feeding monsters, seeing positives in triggers, and so on—point toward befriending our emotions.

Mingyur Rinpoche provides a powerful personal example of befriending emotions. He suffered from full-blown panic disorder until the age of thirteen. When he was thirteen and in the middle of a meditation retreat, Mingyur decided to look deep into his panic. He realized there are two ways to make his panic bigger and stronger: treating it like a boss and obeying its every order, or treating it like an enemy and wishing it to go away. Mingyur decided he would, instead, learn to make friends with panic, neither taking orders from it nor wishing it to go away, but just allowing it to come and go at will and treating it with kindness. In just three days, his panic went away, permanently. "Panic became my best friend, but it was gone in three days, so now I miss my friend," he half-joked to me. Here he describes the insight he gained from this exercise:

> *For three days I stayed in my room meditating. . . . Gradually I began to recognize how feeble and transitory the thoughts and emotions that had troubled me for years actually were, and how fixating on small problems had turned them into big ones. Just by sitting quietly and observing how rapidly, and in many ways illogically, my thoughts and emotions came and went, I began to recognize in a direct way that they weren't nearly as solid or real as they appeared to be. And once I began to let go of my belief in the story they seemed to tell, I began to see the "author" beyond them—the infinitely vast, infinitely open awareness that is the nature of mind itself.*[6]

The great Persian Sufi poet Rumi beautifully describes the mind of befriending emotions in his famous poem, "Guest House":

This being human is a guest house
Every morning a new arrival.

A joy, a depression, a meanness,
some momentary awareness comes
as an unexpected visitor.

Welcome and entertain them all!
Even if they are a crowd of sorrows,
who violently sweep your house
empty of its furniture,

still, treat each guest honorably.
He may be clearing you out
for some new delight.

The dark thought, the shame, the malice,
meet them at the door laughing,
and invite them in.

Be grateful for whoever comes,
because each has been sent
as a guide from beyond.

Inspired by Rumi and Mingyur, and also because I am an engineer pretending to be a poet, I would like to end this chapter with a poem I wrote titled “My Monsters”:

My monsters come in different shapes and sizes.
Over the years, I have learned to deal with them.
I do that by letting go.

First, I let go of my wish to suppress them.
When they arrive, I acknowledge them.
I let them be.

Next, I let go of my instinct to vilify them.
I seek to understand them.

I see them for who they are.
They are merely creations of my body and mind.
I humor them a little.
I joke with them.
I joke about them.
I let them play.

Then, I let go of my desire to feed them.
They may play here all they want.
But they get no food from me.
They are free to stay here hungry, if they want.
I continue to let them be.
Then they get really hungry.
And sometimes they leave.

Finally, I let go of my desire to hold on to them.
They are free to leave as they wish.
I let them go.
I am free.
For now.

I do not overcome them.
They do not overcome me.
And we live together.
In harmony.

"I know they're now good friends with you and all, but must they hang out here so often?"

CHAPTER SIX

Making Profits, Rowing Across Oceans, and Changing the World

The Art of Self-Motivation

The most venerable, clearly understood, enlightened, and reliable constant in the world is not only that we want to be happy, but that we want only to be so. Our very nature requires it of us.

—Saint Augustine

For this chapter to work, we need to enlist a motivation expert. Fortunately, we found that person, and that person is you. You are the world's top expert at figuring out what motivates you. You already know your deepest values and motivations. In this chapter, all we are doing is helping you discover them.

Pleasure, Passion, and Higher Purpose

Tony Hsieh is an inspiration to me. At the young age of twenty-four, Tony sold LinkExchange, the company he cofounded, to Microsoft for $265 million. He later became the CEO of Zappos and grew it from almost nothing to a company with a billion dollars in annual sales. But his entrepreneurial success is not what inspires me. What really inspires me is his wise, skillful, and courageous use of happiness in a corporate setting. Tony figured out that the secret to Zappos' success is "Delivering Happiness", which is also the title of his book. He created a corporate culture that is conducive to employee happiness; happy employees then provide customers the best customer service in the industry, and happy customers spend more money at Zappos. In other words, happiness is not just something nice to have; it is also the centerpiece of Zappos' business strategy and the foundation of its business success. That is really inspiring.

Tony has great insights in the process of happiness in the context of work. He describes three types of happiness: pleasure, passion, and higher purpose.[1]

1. Pleasure: This type of happiness is about always chasing the next high. It is the rock-star type of happiness because it is very hard to maintain unless you are living the lifestyle of a rock star.

2. Passion: Also known as "flow," where peak performance meets peak engagement, and time flies by.

3. Higher Purpose: This is about being part of something bigger than yourself that has meaning to you.

One interesting feature about these three is their varying sustainability. The happiness that arises from pleasure is highly unsustainable. Once the pleasurable stimulus ceases, or if you habituate to it, then your happiness returns to your default set point. Happiness that arises from flow is much more sustainable and you are far less likely to habituate to it. Happiness arising from higher purpose, in contrast, is highly sustainable. In Tony's and also my own experience, this form of happiness is very resilient and can last for a very long time, especially if that higher purpose has an altruistic origin.

Interestingly, we instinctively chase after pleasure believing it to be the source of sustainable happiness. Many of us spend most of our time and energy chasing pleasure, sometimes enjoying flow, and once in a while, we think about higher purpose. Tony's insight suggests we should be doing precisely the reverse. We should be spending most of our time and energy working on higher purpose, sometimes enjoying flow, and every now and then, savoring rock-star pleasure. This is the most logical path toward sustainable happiness, at least in relation to our work.

This insight also suggests the best way to find motivation at work is to find our own higher purpose. If we know what we value most and what is most meaningful to us, then we know what we can work on that serves our higher purpose. When that happens, our work can become a source of sustainable happiness for us. We can then become very good at our work because we are happy doing it, which in turn allows us to enjoy the happiness of flow with increasing frequency. Finally, when we become really good at our work, we may gain recognition. Occasionally, we may even get it in a massive dose, such as a big bonus, a special mention by a company vice president, a story on the *New York Times,* or an expression of gratitude from the Dalai Lama. This is the occasional rock-star pleasure experience that serves as icing on our motivational cake. Once we are working toward fulfilling our higher purpose, the work itself is the reward (but still, the occasional, fat bonus check is very nice, in case you are wondering, boss).

Motivation in Three Easy Steps

In this chapter, we will introduce three practices for motivation:

1. Alignment: Aligning our work with our values and higher purpose

2. Envisioning: Seeing the desired future for ourselves

3. Resilience: The ability to overcome obstacles in our path

Combined, we hope these practices constitute a complete package of tools to help you find out how you want your life to unfold and to navigate the path to get there.

Alignment

Having Fun for a Living

Alignment means aligning our work with our values and higher purpose.

Half jokingly, I think of alignment as finding a way to never have to work again for the rest of your life and still get paid. The secret is to create a situation in which your work is something you do for fun, so you are doing it for your own entertainment anyway and somebody just happens to pay you for it (and since you are nice to them, you do not want to say no to their money). I know of many successful and highly productive people in this situation. Warren Buffett is a famous example, still working . . . er . . . having fun at work in his eighties. Norman Fischer once told me he has never worked a single day in his life, even though he is one of the most sought-after Zen teachers in the country and is busier than most Silicon Valley professionals I know. Closer to home, most of the best engineers I have worked with write code as a hobby, so they really just come to the office to hobby away and get paid.

Work of this nature has at least one of these two qualities, very often both:

1. The work is deeply meaningful to you

2. It generates a state of flow in you

This is, of course, in perfect alignment with Tony Hsieh's pleasure, passion, and higher purpose framework.

Flow

Flow is so important, it is worth mentioning in some detail. Daniel Goleman calls it "the ultimate motivator." Flow is a state of peak performance discovered by Mihaly Csikszentmihalyi, who spent more than two decades studying it in individuals. Csikszentmihalyi describes it as "being completely involved in an activity for its own sake. The ego falls away. Time flies. Every action, movement, and thought follows inevitably from the previous one, like playing jazz. Your whole being is involved, and you're using your skills to the utmost."[2] Athletes know this state as being in the zone. Flow has been reported widely in a very diverse number of fields, such as climbing rocks, performing brain surgery, filing papers, and even in sitting meditation (in fact, one way to think of flow is as Zen in action).

Flow occurs when the task at hand matches the skill level of the practitioner, such that it is difficult enough to provide a challenge but not so difficult that it overwhelms the practitioner. If the task is too easy relative to skill level, the practitioner will be bored or apathetic. In contrast, if it is too difficult, the practitioner becomes anxious or worried. Flow occurs when difficulty is just right.

Flow is a state of focused attention, so people skillful in focusing their attention, such as meditators or martial arts experts, are more likely to find themselves in flow. If you have been doing the mindfulness exercises in the early chapters of this book, you are already halfway there, Grasshopper.

"But this is how I usually improve flow."

Autonomy, Mastery, Purpose

Bestselling author Daniel Pink proposes a framework that is nicely complementary to what we have already discussed. Pink uses fifty years of research in behavioral science to argue that external rewards like money are not the best motivator of high performance; instead, the best motivators are what he calls "intrinsic motivators"—motivation we find within ourselves. The three elements of true motivation are:

1. Autonomy: The urge to direct our own lives
2. Mastery: The desire to get better and better at something that matters

3. Purpose: The yearning to do what we do in service of something larger than ourselves[3]

In his TED talk, Pink tells the fascinating story of research based on the candle problem.[4] The candle problem works like this: participants are given a box of tacks, a candle, and matches. They are asked to find a way to attach the candle to the wall.

Duncker's (1945) Candle Problem:
Subjects are given tacks, a candle and a box of matches and asked to attach the candle to the wall.

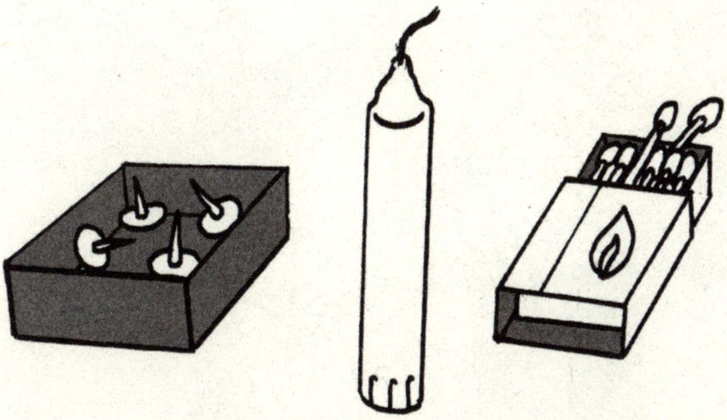

And here's the solution:

It takes a while to figure out the problem, but the solution is fairly simple: empty the box of tacks, attach the candle to the inside of the box, and then attach the box to the wall with a tack. The key creative "aha"

moment needed to solve this problem is figuring out that the box is part of the solution. This is not immediately obvious; you usually begin by thinking of the box merely as something to contain the tacks. So the creative leap here is recognizing the nonobvious use of the box—sort of like thinking outside the box, about the box.

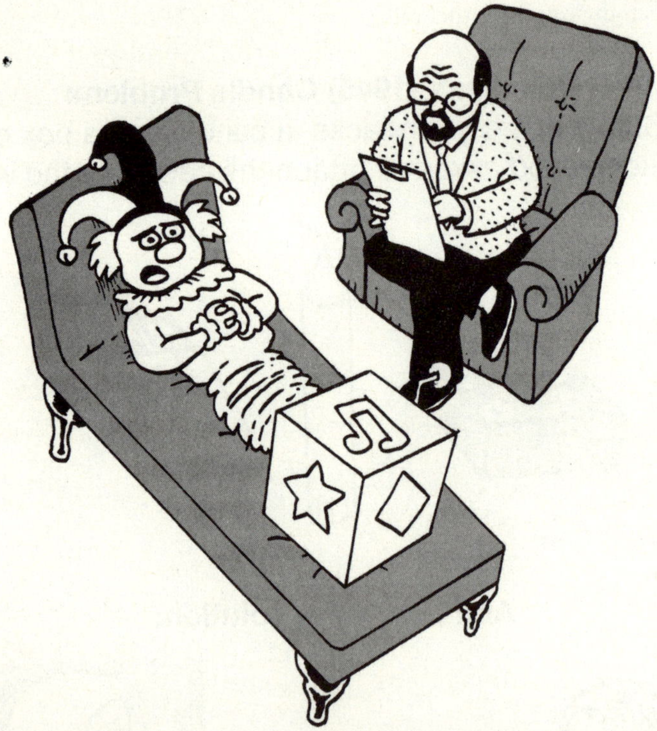

"I'm having real problems thinking outside the box."

Here's the interesting thing: you have two randomly assigned groups. For individuals in one group, the incentivized group, you tell them the faster they can solve this problem, the more money they'll get paid. For individuals in the other group, the control group, you tell them they will get paid the same amount of money regardless of how long they take. Here's the really interesting find: the incentivized group did *worse*! That's right, boys and girls, external incentives not only did not work but were counterproductive.

But wait, the story gets better. In another set of experiments, researchers gave the above items (a box of tacks, a candle, and matches) to participants with the box separate from the tacks. In this case, it is immediately obvious that the box is part of the solution, therefore there is no creative "aha" moment needed. In this case, the incentivized group does better than the control group.

What this and many other similar experiments suggest is traditional monetary incentives work well for routine, rule-based work: jobs that do not require a lot of creativity. For the type of work that requires creativity or other cognitive skills, monetary incentives do not work well; they can even be counterproductive.

For those types of work, the only motivators that work really well are the intrinsic ones: autonomy, mastery, and purpose. In fact, they work so well, they can even turn supposedly soul-deadening jobs into jobs people become proud of. A great example is the customer service team at Zappos. They call themselves the Zappos Customer Loyalty Team (ZCLT). Team members are given very simple instructions: serve the customer, solve the customer's problem, do it the way you want. This, plus attention to employees' professional growth, plus their corporate motto of "delivering happiness," infuses autonomy, mastery, and purpose to the jobs of the ZCLT folks. The result is happy folks delivering customer service that is sometimes rated even more highly than Four Seasons Hotels and Resorts.[5]

Know and Align Thyself

Alignment is built upon self-awareness. When you know yourself at a deep level, you begin to understand your core values, purposes, and priorities. You know what is really important to you and what gives you meaning. With this clarity, you know what makes you happy at work and how best to contribute to the world. You will then know what work situation you want to create for yourself. When the right opportunity presents itself, you will be able to work in ways that offer you autonomy, mastery, and purpose. With that, your work will become a source of your happiness.

The cornerstone of knowing and aligning thyself is mindfulness. Even if you have no other practice than mindfulness alone, you will, over time, create the level of self-awareness you need to find alignment. Mindfulness alone is sufficient—that is the good news.

The better news is there are also other ways to help you clarify your values and higher purpose to yourself. One way is to tell them to other people. Things like values and higher purposes are fairly abstract topics, and the act of verbalizing them forces us to make them clearer and more tangible to ourselves. Another way is to journal. Once again, a similar mechanism is at work—the act of verbalizing abstract thoughts makes them clear and tangible. We find that doing these exercises in a structured way can be very effective. In our class, for example, many participants told us they gained a useful amount of clarity with just a few minutes of speaking to each other.

DISCOVERING VALUES AND HIGHER PURPOSE

If you are doing this alone at home, do a Journaling exercise (see Chapter 4) for a few minutes with one or both of these suggested prompts:

- My core values are . . .
- I stand for . . .

Alternatively, if you have friends or family members to work with (lucky you), do a Mindful Listening exercise (see Chapter 3) in a group of two or three. Take turns to speak. The speaker starts with a monologue, which can be any length, and after that, the group engages in a free conversation when the listeners can ask clarifying questions or make short comments. The only rule during the conversation is the (original) speaker has preemptive priority, which means he or she has priority in speaking and when he or she speaks, nobody can interrupt.

Possible topics of the monologue are:

- What are your core values?
- What do you stand for?

After everybody has a chance to speak, have a meta-conversation to talk about what this experience was like for each of you.

"Core values, core values . . . Hmm . . ."

Envisioning

Envisioning is based on a very simple idea: it's much easier to achieve something if you can visualize yourself already achieving it. Psychiatrist Regina Pally describes it this way:

> *According to neuroscience, even before events happen the brain has already made a prediction about what is most likely to happen,*

> *and sets in motion the perception, behaviors, emotions, physiologic responses and interpersonal ways of relating that best fit with what is predicted. In a sense, we learn from the past what to predict for the future and then live the future we expect.*[6]

Or as Michael Jordan says, "You have to expect things of yourself before you can do them."

In 2005, my friend Roz Savage became the first woman to complete the Atlantic Rowing Race solo. That's right—one woman, one boat, 103 days of rowing across three thousand miles of open ocean. Her cooking stove failed after twenty days and all four of her oars broke, but she made it. But that's just for starters. Roz later became the first woman to row solo across the Pacific Ocean. She did it in three stages. In 2008, she rowed solo from San Francisco to Oahu in Hawaii; in 2009, from Hawaii to Tarawa in Kiribati; and in 2010 to Madang in Papua New Guinea.

Roz wasn't always an adventurer. She insists that before her rowing adventures, she led a normal, comfortable, mostly sedentary, middle-class lifestyle like many of us. She was a management consultant and project manager at an investment bank in London, with a steady income and a house in the suburbs.

Sometime in her midthirties, she did an exercise writing her own obituary. What would people say about her after she died, she wondered. She wrote two versions of her obituary. The first version reflected how things would turn out given her then-current life trajectory. The second version reflected the life she aspired to live. She made a very important discovery during that process. She realized that writing the first version drained so much of her energy, she could not finish it, while she was so energized while writing the second version, she did not want to stop. That was her life-changing insight. She eventually gave up her old life, her job, her steady income, her house, and her marriage to pursue her dream of rowing across oceans.

Some people think Roz must have been wealthy to be able to let go of everything to pursue her dreams. Actually, she wasn't. She told me that when she started rowing across the Atlantic, her entire net worth was her boat and everything inside it (including the cooking stove that eventually broke).

What led Roz to her life-changing insight was an envisioning exercise. It helped her to discover her deepest values and motivations and, at the same time, allowed her to envision her desired future and to consolidate that future in her mind.

"Man, writing my obituary's tougher than I thought."

Discover Your Ideal Future

In Search Inside Yourself, we teach an envisioning practice similar to what Roz did for herself. The basic idea is to envision, discover, and consolidate our ideal future in the mind by writing about it as if it were already true. This is a very powerful practice I learned from my friend Barbara Fittipaldi, president and CEO of the Center for New Futures.

Here are the instructions. Kids, do try this at home; you are experts.

DISCOVERING MY IDEAL FUTURE

This is a writing exercise. We will do this over 7 minutes, which is longer than our usual writing exercises, and there is only one prompt. This exercise can be very fun and fulfilling.

The prompt is:

> If everything in my life, starting from today, meets or exceeds my most optimistic expectations, what will my life be in five years?

The more detailed the imagery in your mind, the better this exercise will work. Hence, consider these questions before writing. In this future:

- Who are you and what are you doing?
- How do you feel?
- What do people say about you?

Let's spend a minute in silent contemplation before writing.

(1-minute pause)

Start writing.

There are variants to this exercise. You can spend more time on it, such as an hour or two instead of seven minutes. Or you can change the destination date; if five years in the future does not work for you, try ten or twenty years. Yet another variation is to pretend you are already living in your ideal future five years from now and to write diary entries from the future. This is the variation we used in Barbara's class.

There are at least two other major variations. One is to write your own obituary, as Roz did, and if you like, write two versions like Roz did. Another is to visualize this scene:

> *You are attending a talk as part of a large audience. Everybody in the audience, including you, is deeply touched and inspired by what the speaker is saying. That speaker is your future self twenty years from now.*

Questions to consider:

- What is the speaker saying and how is it touching and inspiring you?
- What about the speaker makes you look up to him/her?

Talk About Your Ideal Future a Lot

If you find yourself inspired by your ideal future, I highly recommend talking about it a lot to other people. There are two important benefits. First, the more you talk about it, the more real it becomes to you. This works even if your dream is highly improbable or impossible. My own dream, for example, is to create the conditions for world peace in my lifetime. I envision a world that is peaceful because inner peace, inner joy, and compassion are widespread, and those qualities are widespread as a consequence of ancient wisdom practices being made accessible to the modern world. I envision myself as a person who makes wisdom practices accessible by making them understandable, practical, and useful in the corporate world and beyond. When I started thinking about this, I knew my goal was impossible, but I talked about it to a lot of people anyway. The more I talked about it, the more it went from being impossible to implausible, and then from implausible to possible, and more importantly, it went from possible to actionable. I reached a state in my mind in which I felt there were actually things I could do to move it forward.

The second important benefit is the more you talk to people about your ideal future, the more likely you can find people to help you. This is especially true if your aspiration for the future is altruistic in nature because people will rush to help you. If your wish is to drive a nice Lexus, nobody will care. However, if your wish is something altruistic—for example, you want to feed every hungry person in the world, or you want to make sure no homeless person in San Francisco ever dies from the cold, or you aspire to help disadvantaged kids in your community learn better—and you are sincere about your wish to serve others, I guarantee the most common response will be, "How can I help?" When you are genuinely moved to help others, you inspire people with your altruism, and when you inspire them, they want to help you.

Truth be told, I was actually surprised by how well it worked. When I first started talking to others about my aspirations for world peace, I was pleasantly surprised how few people thought I was crazy (only two, so far). As it became more real to me, I began speaking about it with increasing confidence and, after a while, I noticed that people wanted to help me or introduce other people to me who could help me.

Soon, I was building a network of allies (whom I jokingly call the "grand conspiracy for world peace"). I found myself befriending many luminaries of the contemplative world such as Matthieu Ricard, and luminaries in the peace-making world like Scilla Elworthy. Richard Gere and the Dalai Lama gave me hugs. Owen Wilson and will.i.am said they wanted to help me. I was invited to deliver a TED talk on compassion at the United Nations. Many hundreds of strangers tell me that I have inspired them. I am amazed by how much my simple aspiration for world peace has resonated with so many people, and I am humbled by all the friendship and kindness I have experienced.

I learned that people want to be inspired. Every aspiration of service we have and every act of charity we perform inspires others. Hence, if you have altruistic aspirations, especially if you are already acting on them, I very much encourage you to share them with others so you can inspire more goodness in the world.

Resilience

Resilience is the ability to overcome obstacles along the way. Alignment and envisioning help you find out where you want to go, and resilience helps you get there.

We can train resilience on three levels:

1. Inner calm: Once we can consistently access the inner calm in the mind, it becomes the foundation of all optimism and resilience.

2. Emotional resilience: Success and failure are emotional experiences. By working at this level, we can increase our capacity for them.

3. Cognitive resilience: Understanding how we explain our setbacks to ourselves and creating useful mental habits help us develop optimism.

Inner Calm

I once asked Matthieu Ricard the most obvious question one can ever ask of the happiest man in the world. The question was: are there ever days when you are not happy?

Like most wise masters you see in Chinese kung fu movies, Matthieu answered with a metaphor: "Think of happiness as a deep ocean. The surface may be choppy, but the bottom is always calm. Similarly, there are days when a deeply happy person may feel sad—for example, he sees people suffering—but underneath that sadness, there is a large depth of unwavering happiness."

This lovely metaphor also works for calmness and resilience. If you have access to a deep inner calm in your mind, then no matter the ups and downs of day-to-day life, you can always be resilient. Nothing can get you down for a prolonged period of time because every time something beats you down, you can always rest and recover in that inner calm and, depending on how deep your practice is, bounce back quickly.

Fortunately, this inner calm is accessible to everyone. As we mentioned in Chapters 2 and 3, by training in mindfulness, the mind can become calm, clear, and happy, and the more we practice mindfulness, the more the mind becomes so.

Just do a lot of mindfulness meditation, and this aspect will be "automagically" taken care of.

Emotional Resilience

Success and failure are emotional experiences. These emotions can give rise to grasping and aversion, which can hold us back and hamper our ability to achieve our goals. We can build upon the foundations of inner calm with practices that help us deal with the emotions involved in success and failure.

Like all emotional experiences, success and failure manifest most strongly in our bodies. Therefore, the place to start working on those emotions is in the body. The idea is to become comfortable with experiencing these emotions in our bodies, or in the words of Mingyur Rinpoche, making them our friends. We also let go of any grasping or aversion that arises. When we become capable of containing the emotions and able to let go of grasping and aversion, we can become emotionally resilient to success and failure.

In formal practice in Search Inside Yourself, we begin by calming the mind and doing a quick body scan, and then bringing up memories of failure and success. In each case, we experience them in our bodies, letting go of grasping and aversion. Here are the instructions:

MEDITATION ON RESILIENCE

Calming the Mind

Start with 3 deep breaths.

Bring gentle awareness to the breath, becoming aware of the in and out breaths, and the spaces in between.

(continued)

Let's bring attention to our bodies, beginning by focusing on sensations in the feet, legs, knees, pelvis, chest, arms, shoulders, back, neck, back of head, and face.

(Long pause)

Failure

Let's now shift gears into an experience of failure for 4 minutes.

Bring to mind a memory of an event when you experienced a sense of significant failure—not having met your goal, having let yourself and others down. See, hear, and feel it.

Observe all the associated emotions and see how they manifest in the body.

(2-minute pause)

Let us see if we can create the ability to experience all those emotions without aversion.

Consider these emotions you are experiencing as simply physiological sensations. That is all. They may be unpleasant, but they are simply experiences. Let's simply allow these experiences to be present, to come as they wish, and to go as they wish. Just let them be, in a kind, gentle, generous way.

(Long pause)

Success

Let's now have more fun and shift gears into an experience of success for 4 minutes.

Bring to mind a memory of an event when you experienced a sense of significant success—having exceeded your goal, being admired by all, feeling great about yourself. See, hear, and feel it.

Observe all the associated emotions and see how they manifest in the body.

(2-minute pause)

Let us see if we can create the ability to experience all those emotions without grasping.

Consider these emotions you are experiencing as simply physiological sensations. That is all. They may be very pleasant, but they are simply experiences. Let's simply allow these experiences to be present, to come as they wish, and to go as they wish. Just let them be, in a kind, gentle, generous way.

(Long pause)

Returning to Calm

Let us now return to the present for 3 minutes. Check in with your body and how it feels now.

(Pause)

Take a deep breath and let go. Continue a relaxed attention on breathing and, if you feel so inclined, bring a hand up to rest on the chest.

(Pause)

Continue noticing what happens in your body, and slowly open your eyes.

Thank you for your attention.

Cognitive Resilience

We can further build upon emotional resilience with cognitive training that develops optimism. Let's start with a story of failure.

Once upon a time, there was an athlete who was brave enough to tell the world how much of a failure he was:

> *"I've missed more than nine thousand shots in my career. I've lost almost three hundred games. Twenty-six times I've been trusted to take the game-winning shot and missed. I've failed over and over and over again in my life. . . ."*

And he continued,

> *". . . and that is why I succeed."*[7]

The athlete's name is Michael Jordan, and for those of you who don't know of him, well, he is only the greatest basketball player of all time.

Failure is the building block of success. Soichiro Honda famously said, "Success is 99 percent failure." Thomas Watson said, "If you want to increase your success rate, double your failure rate." There is even a popular Chinese proverb that says, "Failure is the mother of success." (I would hate to be the mom in that family, though).

If you dislike failure, the story gets worse. If you want to do something new and innovative, you often need to feel stupid as well. This point was made by Nathan Myhrvold (talking about his friend Bill Gates but also making a general point about going outside the box):

> *Lewis and Clark were lost most of the time. If your idea of exploration is to always know where you are and to be inside your zone of competence, you don't do wild new shit. You have to be confused, upset, think you're stupid. If you're not willing to do that, you can't go outside the box.*[8]

Nathan Myhrvold completed his Ph.D. at the age of twenty-three. He was the chief technology officer at Microsoft and the founder of Microsoft Research. He was a prize-winning nature and wildlife photographer and master French chef, and he co-authored a bestselling book. He must be one of the most intelligent human beings on this earth. Even Bill Gates said, "I don't know anyone I would say is smarter than Nathan." Yet, even for Nathan Myhrvold and Bill Gates, innovating involves being "confused, upset, think[ing] you're stupid." Reading that quote made me feel better about myself because if even Nathan Myhrvold is capable of feeling stupid, I can excuse myself for doing so.

The evidence above confirms something a lot of us have already learned from our own lives: that failure is a common experience. Everybody fails in some major way at some point in their lives, even the greatest and most successful among us, like Michael Jordan. What distinguishes successful people is their attitude toward failure, and specifically, how they explain their own failures to themselves.

Martin Seligman, the highly esteemed father of learned optimism, calls it the "explanatory style"—how we talk to ourselves when we experience a setback. People who are optimistic react to setbacks from a presumption of personal power. They feel that setbacks are temporary, are isolated to particular circumstances, and can eventually be overcome by effort and abilities. In contrast, people who are pessimistic react to setbacks from a presumption of personal helplessness. They feel that setbacks are long lasting, generalized across their lives, and are due to their own inadequacies, and therefore cannot be overcome. This difference in how we explain occurrences to ourselves has a profound impact on our lives. When an optimist suffers a major disappointment, he responds by figuring out how he can do it better the next time. In contrast, a pessimist assumes there is nothing he can do about the problem and gives up.

In a series of famous experiments done in collaboration with MetLife, Seligman discovered that optimistic insurance agents significantly outsell their pessimistic counterparts.[9] What's more, MetLife had a chronic shortage of agents, so Seligman convinced MetLife to hire a special group of applicants who scored just below the cutoff point on the normal screening test but scored high on optimism. This group outsold the pessimists in the group of regular hires by 21 percent in their first year and 57 percent in their second year!

Learning Optimism, Unlearning Pessimism

Happily, optimism is something that can be learned. Ironically enough, optimism starts with being realistic and objective. We naturally pay much more attention to negative than positive occurrences in our lives. For example, if you're a writer and out of ten reviews of your work, nine are glowing and one is nasty, chances are you will remember that one nasty review more than the glowing ones. This is also true for other aspects of our lives. Barbara Fredrickson, a noted pioneer in positive psychology, found that it takes three positive experiences to overcome a negative one, a 3:1 ratio.[10] In general, each negative feeling is three times as powerful as a positive one. If you put that in perspective for a moment, let's assume you live a life in which you have twice as many happy moments as unhappy ones, a 2:1 ratio. It is like some rich uncle gives you two dollars for every dollar somebody else takes from you. Dude, you win! Objectively, it would look as if you are very lucky and have a very good life. Subjectively, however, since your 2:1 ratio is still well below Fredrickson's 3:1 ratio, you would think, "My life sucks." This insight hit me like three Zen sticks hitting my head (yes, a 3:1 stick-to-head ratio).

The first step to learning optimism is becoming aware of our own strong negative experiential bias. It is entirely possible, even likely, that we have much more success than failure in our lives, yet it does not seem that way because we pay too much attention to our failures and too little attention to our successes. Just understanding this can change how you see yourself.

The second step is mindfulness. Learning optimism requires us to create objectivity toward our own experiences and, as mentioned in Chapter 4, mindfulness is the best way to create that objectivity. Specifically, whenever you experience success or failure, first bring mindfulness to your body. Next, bring mindfulness to the emotional experience, remembering that the body is where emotions manifest most vividly. Finally, bring mindfulness to your thoughts. How are you explaining the event to yourself? Do you feel powerful or helpless? How are your thoughts related to your emotions? If this event is an experience of success, bring mindfulness to the tendency to downplay it, or if the event is an experience of failure, bring mindfulness to its disproportionally strong effect on you.

The final step is transformation. When experiencing success, take conscious note of it and accept credit for it. This creates a mental habit of paying due attention to your successes. When experiencing failure, focus on realistic evidence suggesting that this setback may be temporary. If you have thoughts of inadequacy, recall past successes of which you took conscious note and for which you accepted credit. If you find any evidence suggesting reasons for realistic hope, bring attention to it. This sounds a bit like denial, but what it actually does is to increase objectivity by balancing out your natural, strong negative bias. Doing this often creates new mental habits so the next time you experience failure, your mind will quickly find realistic reasons for hope and you can recover more quickly from your setback. And thus, optimism is created.

Great Waves

We end this chapter with a story of a Japanese man who overcame his fear and failure by discovering his inner resilience.

> *In the early days of the Meiji era there lived a well-known wrestler called O-nami, Great Waves.*

O-nami was immensely strong and knew the art of wrestling. In his private bouts he defeated even his teacher, but in public, he was so bashful that his own pupils beat him.

O-nami felt he should go to a Zen master for help. Hakuju, a wandering teacher, was stopping in a little temple nearby, so O-nami went to see him and told him of his great trouble.

"Great Waves is your name," the teacher advised, "so stay in this temple tonight. Imagine that you are those billows. You are no longer a wrestler who is afraid. You are those huge waves sweeping everything before them, swallowing all in their path. Do this and you will be the greatest wrestler in the land."

The teacher retired. O-nami sat in meditation trying to imagine himself as waves. He thought of many different things. Then gradually he turned more and more to the feeling of waves. As the night advanced the waves became larger and larger. They swept away the flowers in their vases. Even the Buddha in the shrine was inundated. Before dawn, the temple was nothing but the ebb and flow of an immense sea.

In the morning, the teacher found O-nami meditating, a faint smile on his face. He patted the wrestler's shoulder. "Now nothing can disturb you," he said. "You are those waves. You will sweep everything before you."

The same day O-nami entered the wrestling contests and won. After that, no one in Japan was able to defeat him.[11]

"Watch it, boys, here comes the new coach, and he looks like a mean sonofagun!"

CHAPTER SEVEN

Empathy and the Monkey Business of Brain Tangos

Developing Empathy Through Understanding and Connecting with Others

Seek first to understand, then to be understood.

—Stephen R. Covey

Here is a joke I came across a long time ago.

Once upon a time, a disciple asked, "Master, is half the holy life associating with people?"

The master replied, "No, the *whole* of holy life is associating with people."

This joke probably started as a misreading of a famous Buddhist story in which the Buddha told Ananda that friendships with "admirable people" are not half of holy life, but the whole of holy life. Over time, however, I found the humorous apocryphal version to be deeply insightful. In the context of emotional intelligence, I think that associating with people is where the proverbial rubber meets the road ("Hi rubber!" "Hello road!").

So, congratulations on completing the intrapersonal intelligence chapters of this book, and welcome to interpersonal intelligence—black-belt territory.

Empathy, the Brain, and Monkey Business

I find it very funny that one of the most important discoveries in neuroscience was accidentally made when somebody picked up food in front of a monkey.

A group of neurophysiologists at the University of Parma, Italy, placed electrodes in a monkey's brain to record neural activity.[1] They found that some neurons fired every time the monkey picked up a piece of food. As part of the monkey business of science, researchers sometimes had to pick up food to give to the monkey, and when they did, they were surprised to find those same neurons fired in the monkey's brain. Further investigation revealed the existence of something called "mirror neurons." These are brain cells that fire both when the animal is performing an activity and *also* when it watches another animal perform the same activity. Not surprisingly, evidence was later discovered that strongly suggested the human brain contains these mirror neurons as well.

Some scientists suggest that mirror neurons form the neural basis of empathy and social cognition. The scientific evidence backing that claim is not (yet) conclusive, but either way, mirror neurons offer a fascinating glimpse into the social nature of the human brain. It is as if the brain was designed with other people in mind (excuse the pun), right down to the level of individual neurons.[2]

Another fascinating glimpse into empathy at the neural level is revealed by the way the brain reacts to the pain of other people. When you are given a painful stimulus, parts of your brain nicknamed the "pain matrix" light up. If, instead of receiving the painful stimulus, you observe a loved one receiving it, your own pain matrix still lights up.[3] In a very real way, in your brain, you are experiencing their suffering. You do not necessarily experience the same sensory input, but you share a similar affective experience. This is the neural foundation of compassion. The very word *compassion* comes from the Latin words for "suffering together." Even without us putting in any effort, our brains are already pre-wired for empathy and compassion, at least for loved ones.

Brain Tango

There is a fascinating relationship between self-awareness and empathy. If you are strong in self-awareness, you are also very likely to be strong in empathy. The brain seems to use the same equipment for both tasks. Specifically, both qualities seem to have a lot to do with the part of the brain known as the insula. The insula is related to the ability to experience and recognize bodily sensations. People with very active insulae, for example, can become aware of their own heartbeats. What is really interesting is scientific evidence suggesting that people with active insulae also tend to have high empathy.[4]

How does that work? The work of famed psychologist John Gottman and his collaborators offers an interesting hint. Gottman is famous for his pioneering work on marital stability and relationship analysis. His expertise is legendary, and he is reputed to be able to accurately predict if a marriage will end in divorce within ten years just by observing a fifteen-minute conversation between the couple. Much of Gottman's research work involves getting a couple into a room, hooking them up to equipment that records their physiological signals, and getting the couple to talk to each other (for example, about a topic on which they disagree) while being videotaped. Later, each spouse also watches the video separately and rates how he or she felt during each stage of the conversation. These experiments yield a treasure trove of data, with a videotape of each conversation, first-person ratings of how each participant felt during the conversation, and physiological data.

In an interesting experiment, Gottman's collaborator, Robert Levenson, had a third subject (let's call her the "rater") view some of the videos from above and rate how one of the subjects in the video felt at each stage during the conversation.[5] In this experiment, the empathy of the rater was measured: the more accurately the rater rated the feeling of the subject, the more empathy she demonstrated. The most interesting part of this experiment concerned the rater's physiological signals, which were also measured during the session. The finding: the better the rater's physiology matched the target's, the more accurately she rated the target's feelings.

"Really? What gives you the idea that my husband is capable of empathy?"

In other words, empathy works by having you physiologically mimic the other person. The word Daniel Goleman uses to describe this phenomenon is *entrainment.*[6] He also calls it an "emotional tango." Entrainment is the reason empathy is so closely related to self-awareness: the brain uses its self-awareness equipment for empathy. In fact, you can even say that empathy relies on self-awareness, and if our self-awareness is weak, our empathy will be weak too.

One important implication of this insight is that, oftentimes, practices that develop self-awareness also simultaneously develop empathy. For example, bringing mindful attention to your body (for instance, using the Body Scan exercise in Chapter 4) is known to strengthen the insula, and by doing so, it improves both self-awareness and empathy at the same time. Two for the price of one!

Empathy Is Not Psychologizing or Agreeing

Empathy is often confused with something called "psychologizing," or speculating in psychological terms or on psychological motivations, often in an uninformed way. For example, let's say you are explaining your problems to your boss, and midway through, your boss interrupts you to explain how your problems have to do with your presumed childhood issues and some other things he might have read about in pop psychology. He is psychologizing, not empathizing. When we psychologize, we are actually dismissing the problem, not understanding it. Unsurprisingly, psychologizing has been linked to mediocre performance in managers. I imagine that managers who psychologize routinely may start growing pointy hair like Dilbert's pointy-haired boss. If, instead, your boss listens intently to you with his full attention, tries to understand what your problem means to you at both a cognitive and a visceral level, and does all that with kindness, he is empathizing.

"I'm demoting you because you have unresolved issues with your mother."

Empathy does not necessarily mean agreeing. It is possible to understand another person at both an intellectual and a visceral level with kindness, and still respectfully disagree. Aristotle said, "It is the mark of an educated mind to be able to entertain a thought without accepting it." Disagreeing with empathy is a lot like that. It is the mark of a developed mind to be able to understand and accept another's feeling without agreeing to it.

That insight suggests that it is possible to make tough decisions while still being empathetic. In fact, in many situations, the best way to make tough decisions is with kindness and empathy. In a business setting, if we have to make a decision that hurts somebody's interest, it is easy to tell ourselves not to bring empathy to the situation, because if we do, we will just make it hard for ourselves to make our tough, but necessary, decision. I found this to be suboptimal. If we make tough decisions without empathy, we can more easily achieve what we want in the short term, but we also create resentment and mistrust, which hurt our own interests in the long term. If instead we treat the affected people with kindness and empathy, we create trust and understanding. With that, we may become more able to skillfully negotiate and manage their concerns. With enough trust and understanding, we may even be able to find creative ways that either solve everybody's problems or at least mitigate some concerns in some major way. In sum, tough decisions still need to be made, but if people trust you, feel that your heart is in the right place, and understand that you are doing this for the greater good, you are more likely to win their cooperation. Better still, once trust is established, it becomes a foundation upon which you can build a strong long-term working relationship. Hence, you win in both the short and long term.

A great example of making difficult decisions with empathy is found in Goleman's *Working with Emotional Intelligence:*

> *Consider how employees were treated when plants closed at two companies. At GE, workers had two years' notice that the plant would be closed, and the company made an intense outplacement effort to help*

them find other jobs. The other company announced the closing with just one week's notice, and made no effort to help workers locate other employment.

The results? Almost a year later, the majority of the former GE workers said it had been a good place to work, and 93 percent lauded the transition services offered them. At the other company, only 3 percent said it had been a good place to work. GE preserved a large pool of goodwill, while the other firm left a legacy of bitterness.

When we lay people off, we are subjecting them to one of the most painful experiences in their lives. Yet it is possible to do even that with empathy, and even under those painful circumstances, trust and goodwill can be created. Some people call it "being tough without being an SOB."

How to Increase Empathy

Empathy increases with kindness. Kindness is the engine of empathy; it motivates you to care, and it makes you more receptive to others, and them to you. The more kindness you offer to people, the better you can empathize with them.

Empathy also increases with perceived similarity. The more we perceive somebody to be just like us, the more we empathize with him or her. There is a fascinating study by Andrea Serino and team, aptly titled *I Feel What You Feel If You Are Similar to Me,* which hints at how powerful the perception of similarity can be for empathy.[7] The study is based on the discovery that watching a video of your own body being touched can temporarily increase your sensitivity to touch. For example, if your cheeks are electrically stimulated at an intensity just below what you can perceive (called "subthreshold tactile stimuli"), you probably will not feel it. But if it happens at the same time you see a video of your cheeks being touched, you probably will feel it. In other words, watching your cheeks being touched makes you more sensitive to feeling your cheeks being touched. This mechanism is called "visual remapping of touch," and it also works if you observe a video of another person's face being touched instead of your own face. Amazing stuff.

Serino's study explored the question of whether this visual remapping of touch works better if the face you see being touched belongs to someone you consider to be similar to you. In the first experiment, they used faces from each participant's own ethnic group versus those from another ethnic group (in this case, Caucasian versus Maghrebian). Fascinatingly, but perhaps not surprisingly, it turned out to work measurably better for faces belonging to each participant's own ethnic group.

The second experiment used faces from the leadership of each participant's political party versus those from the opposing political party (all from the same ethnic group). Results show this visual remapping to work measurably better if the face comes from one's own political party! This is jaw dropping. The mere perception of whether or not a person shares your political beliefs can measurably affect how you respond to him at an unconscious, neurological level.

Hence, to become more empathetic, we need to create a mind that instinctively responds to everyone with kindness and an automatic perception of others being "just like me." In other words, we need to create mental habits.

Creating Desired Mental Habits

The practice of creating mental habits is based on a simple, intuitively obvious yet profoundly important insight. The Buddha describes it this way:

> *Whatever one frequently thinks and ponders upon, that will become the inclination of his mind.*[8]

In other words, what we think, we become.

The method itself is simple; invite a thought to arise in your mind often enough, and it will become a mental habit. For example, if every time you see another person, you wish for that person to be happy, then eventually, it will become your mental habit and whenever you meet another person, your instinctive first thought is to wish for that person to be happy. After a while, you develop an instinct for kindness. You become a kind person. Your kindness shows in your face, posture, and attitude every time you meet somebody. People will become attracted to your personality, not just your good looks.

The informal way to practice is simply to generate these thoughts every time you meet people. However, there is also a formal, systematic way of doing it, which many people find highly effective. We call it the Just Like Me / Loving Kindness practice.

Just Like Me / Loving Kindness Practice

There are two separate practices for seeing similarity and offering kindness. The first is a practice called Just Like Me, in which we remind ourselves how similar other people are to us, thereby creating the mental habit of equality. The second is a popular practice called Loving Kindness Meditation, where we create good wishes for others, thereby creating the mental habit of kindness. We combine both practices into one.

In class, we often do this exercise in pairs with participants sitting facing each other. For our purpose here, instead of finding somebody to sit down facing you, simply visualize somebody you care about in your mind while doing the exercise.

I urge you to read the scripts for Just Like Me and Loving Kindness slowly and with generous amounts of pause.

JUST LIKE ME AND LOVING KINDNESS MEDITATION

Setup

Sit in a comfortable position that allows you to be alert and relaxed at the same time. Start with 2 minutes to rest the mind on the breath.

Bring to mind somebody you care about. Visualize him or her. If you wish, you may use a photograph or video of that person.

Just Like Me

Now, read the script below slowly to yourself, pausing at the end of each sentence for reflection:

This person has a body and a mind, just like me.

This person has feelings, emotions, and thoughts, just like me.

(continued)

This person has, at some point in his or her life, been sad, disappointed, angry, hurt, or confused, just like me.

This person has, in his or her life, experienced physical and emotional pain and suffering, just like me.

This person wishes to be free from pain and suffering, just like me.

This person wishes to be healthy and loved, and to have fulfilling relationships, just like me.

This person wishes to be happy, just like me.

Loving Kindness

Now, let's allow some wishes to arise.

I wish for this person to have the strength, the resources, and the emotional and social support to navigate the difficulties in life.

I wish for this person to be free from pain and suffering.

I wish for this person to be happy.

Because this person is a fellow human being, just like me.

(Pause)

Now, I wish for everybody I know to be happy.

(Long pause)

Closing

End with 1 minute of resting the mind.

Whenever we've asked participants how they felt during the exercise, the most common response has been "happy." They discovered that being on the transmitting end of kindness is a calming and happy experience, often at least as good as being on the receiving end. This seems a little counterintuitive, but it makes sense once you remember we are highly social creatures and even our brains are pre-wired to be social. Given how social we are and how social we need to be to survive, it makes sense for kindness toward other people to be intrinsically rewarding to ourselves; it is probably an important part of our survival mechanism. One study even suggests that performing one kind act a day over just ten days can measurably increase your happiness.[9]

In other words, **kindness is a sustainable source of happiness**—a simple yet profound insight that can change lives.

"Are you sure this is how you're supposed to do this Just Like Me exercise?"

How to Save Your Marriage and Other Relationships

One of the best things about the above practice is it can be used in any situation to heal relationships. I've found it extremely useful for dealing with conflicts. Whenever I have a fight with my wife or a co-worker, I go to another room to calm down and after a few minutes of calming down, I do this exercise in stealth. I visualize the other person in the next room. I remind myself that this person is just like me, wants to be free from suffering just like me, wants to be happy just like me, and so on. And then I wish that person wellness, happiness, freedom from suffering, and so on. After just a few minutes of doing this, I feel much better about myself, about the other person, and about the whole situation. A large part of my anger dissipates immediately.

The next time you get into conflict with someone you care about or someone you work with, I suggest doing this practice. It may do wonders for your relationships. I reckon this practice is a major reason being married to me does not totally suck.

Traditional Practice of Loving Kindness

The Loving Kindness practice above is our adaptation of an old practice called Metta Bhavana, or Loving Kindness Meditation. The traditional form of the practice is a little more structured and moves at a slower pace (which is funny, since I am an engineer and my adaptation of it is to make it *less* structured).

Like every other meditation practice, the traditional Metta Bhavana starts with a few minutes of resting the mind. Once some mental calmness is established, you invite a feeling of kindness toward yourself. To do this, quietly repeat these phrases to yourself:

> May I be well.
>
> May I be happy.
>
> May I be free from suffering.

After a few minutes of this, invite a feeling of kindness toward someone you already like or admire, someone for whom it is easy to create loving kindness. If you like, you may use the above phrases for that person. May he or she be well, happy, and free from suffering.

After a few minutes of that, do the same for a neutral person, or somebody you do not particularly like or dislike, or whom you may not even know particularly well. A few minutes later, do it toward a difficult person, or somebody you dislike or who creates a lot of difficulty in your life. May he or she be well, happy, and free from suffering. Finally, extend the feeling to all sentient beings. May all sentient beings be well, happy, and free from suffering.

One of the best things about this traditional form is that by the time you get to the difficult person, your mind has already marinated in loving kindness, making it easier for you to break your mental habits about that particular person. For example, if your mental habit is to naturally generate a feeling of dislike every time you think of Rick, and you use Rick as the object of Metta Bhavana every day, after a while, your mind may start to associate Rick with a positive feeling since every time you think of Rick in that meditation, your mind has been soaked in loving kindness. After a while, you may find yourself no longer disliking Rick, and you may have to find a new difficult person for Metta Bhavana. (Eventually, you may even run out of people you dislike, which can be annoying for the purpose of this meditation, but is not a bad problem to have, really).

Feel free to use this traditional practice if it works better for you.

Bringing Out the Best in People

In the previous sections, we learned practices for developing foundational empathy skills. In the next few sections, let us focus on practices that help us facilitate the growth of others and bring out the best in them.

Establishing Trust Is Good for Work

Empathy is nice, but it is not just nice; it is also essential for helping you succeed at your work, especially if your work involves building a team or coaching, mentoring, and caring for others. There is one basic ability that enables you to be highly effective at those activities, and that is your ability to establish trust. Trust me on that one.

Empathy helps us build trust. When we interact with empathy, we increase the likelihood that people feel seen, heard, and understood. When people feel those things, they feel safer and more likely to trust the person who understands them.

Key thinkers on effectiveness at work have trust as the foundation of their practices and approaches. For example, Marc Lesser, an accomplished executive coach, suggests the coaching/mentoring cycle to involve these steps:

1. Establish trust.
2. Listen (by "looping" and "dipping").
3. Ask probing and open-ended questions.
4. Provide feedback.
5. Partner to create options and practices.

The most important step is the first step, establishing trust. Trust is the foundation of a coaching/mentoring relationship. It is very simple:

for you to work with your mentee, he must be open to you. The more he opens himself up, the more effectively you can work with him, and the more he trusts you, the more likely he is to be open. It is that simple. If there is no trust, this mentoring relationship will just be a waste of time (unless you are having doughnuts during your mentoring conversations, in which case the doughnuts make up for some of the time wasted, but this is not a suggestion to replace trust with doughnuts).

Similarly, trust is the essential foundation of a highly effective team. In *The Five Dysfunctions of a Team,* Patrick Lencioni describes five ways a team becomes dysfunctional in the form of a pyramid.[10]

The five dysfunctions, in order of causality are:

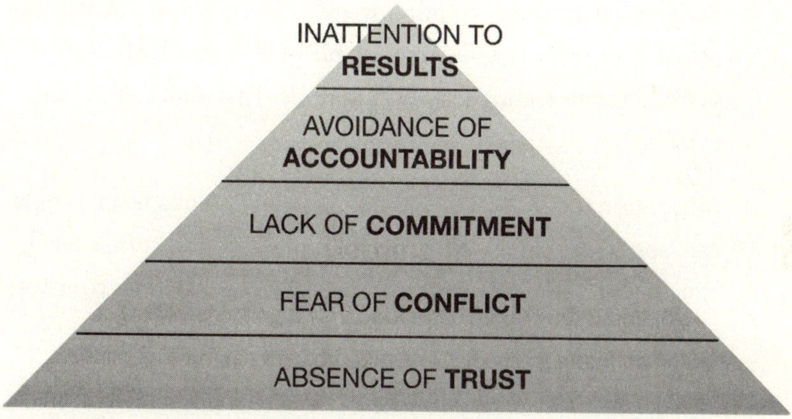

1. Absence of trust: People do not trust the intentions of their teammates. They feel the need to protect themselves from each other and tread carefully around others on the team. This leads to the next dysfunction.
2. Fear of conflict: Without trust, people are unwilling to involve themselves in productive debates and conflicts, the type of good

conflict that focuses entirely on resolving issues without involving character attacks or hidden personal agendas. Without such healthy conflicts, issues stay unresolved or are unsatisfactorily resolved. People feel they have not been properly involved in decisions. This leads to the next dysfunction.

3. Lack of commitment: When people feel their input has not been properly considered and that they have not been properly involved in decisions, they have no buy in. They do not commit to the final decisions. Ambiguity about priorities and directions festers, and uncertainties linger. This leads to the next dysfunction.

4. Avoidance of accountability: When people have no buy in about decisions, they avoid accepting accountability. Worse still, they do not hold their teammates accountable to high standards. Resentment festers, and mediocrity spreads. This leads to the final dysfunction.

5. Inattention to results: The ultimate dysfunction of a team. People care about something other than the collective goals of the team. Goals are not met, results are not achieved, and you lose your best people to your competitors.

It all begins with trust. The absence of trust is the root cause of all other dysfunctions. Specifically, the type of trust Lencioni talks about is what he calls "vulnerability-based trust." That is when team members trust the intentions of each other enough that they are willing to expose their own vulnerabilities because they are confident their exposed vulnerabilities will not be used against them. Hence, they are willing to admit issues and deficiencies and ask for help. In other words, they are able to concentrate their energies on achieving the team's common goals, rather than wasting time trying to defend their egos and look good to their teammates.

"Actually, Dave, we were kind of hoping we could go back to when you didn't feel so open about exposing all your vulnerabilities to us."

This vulnerability-based trust is the same type of trust Marc Lesser talks about as being the foundation of an effective mentoring/coaching relationship. Once you learn to establish this type of trust, you can become effective not just as a team leader but also as a mentor and coach.

Start with Sincerity, Kindness, and Openness

Many years ago, I had a manager, John, whom I like and respect a lot. John and I became good personal friends. John left the company we worked for under very unpleasant circumstances, which were very unfair to him, in my opinion. When a new manager, Eric, came in to replace John, I was not happy. Emotionally, I felt resentment toward Eric, but cognitively, I knew it really was not Eric's fault. So I decided to dissolve all my resentment toward him. By then, I was already a seasoned meditator, so I knew precisely which tool to use: empathy.

Eric was already an acquaintance of mine and I occasionally worked with him on small things, so I knew he was not a bad person. In fact, cognitively, I suspected (correctly, it turned out) that he was a good person, and all I had to do was convince my emotional brain. So during our first one-on-one meeting with him as my manager, I made sure to only talk about personal stuff and to do so with kindness and openness. We exchanged life stories and aspirations. I asked him how he wanted to save the world. The purpose of doing all that was to allow both my cognitive brain and my emotional brain a chance to know Eric as a human being, and to associate him with his inner goodness, so that every time I saw him, my emotional brain would react with, "This is a good man. I like him."

It worked like a charm. Eric earned my trust immediately by reciprocating my sincerity, kindness, and openness. Better still, I found him to be a very good and admirable person. He had, for example, spent much of his youth doing peace-building work in third-world countries, something he hardly ever talks about but which I enormously respect. By the end of our first conversation, my emotional brain was placated and my thinking brain got to tell my emotional brain, "See? I *told* you he is a good person!" My resentment toward him completely dissolved.

Within the space of a single one-hour conversation, Eric and I established a strong foundation for mutual trust. We had a very positive and productive working relationship for the rest of the time we worked together, and I am happy to call him my friend.

(True story, names have been changed to protect me.)

The moral of the story is to always have doughnuts at meetings. No, I am just kidding. The real moral of the story is that trust has to begin with sincerity, kindness, and openness, so it is optimally productive to start every relationship that way, both in work and in life. Whenever possible, begin by assuming that the other person is a good person and deserves to be treated as such, until proven otherwise.

The other lesson is that it is useful to always engage the other person as a human being. When establishing trust, I find that my cognitive brain is usually easy to deal with—the hard part is placating my emotional brain. To placate the emotional brain, I must recognize that the other person is a human being just like me. The other person is not just a negotiating opponent or a customer or a co-worker; he is also a human being, just like me. When your mind can operate at that level in every situation, especially in difficult situations, you create strong conditions for mutual trust.

Dr. Karen May, Google's vice president of leadership and talent—and the most empathetic person I have ever worked with—offers two additional tips for building trust:

1. Practice giving people the benefit of the doubt: Most people do what they do because it feels like the right thing at the time, based on what they want to accomplish and the information they have. Their reasons make sense to them, even if their actions do not make sense to us. Assume that they are making the right choice, even if we do not understand it or might make a different choice ourselves.

2. Remember that trust begets trust: One way I can build trust with you is to assume that you are trustworthy and to treat you that way. When you feel that someone trusts you, it makes it easier to trust them back, and vice versa.

"Will it work even with mothers-in-law?"

Three Assumptions

Whenever I chair a meeting, I like to begin with a practice I call the Three Assumptions: I invite everybody in the meeting room to make the following assumptions about everybody else:

1. Assume that everybody in this room is here to serve the greater good, until proven otherwise.
2. Given the above assumption, we therefore assume that none of us has any hidden agenda, until proven otherwise.
3. Given the above assumption, we therefore assume that we are all reasonable even when we disagree, until proven otherwise.

I find that when you begin a meeting with these assumptions, there is a greater sense of trust in the room. I recommend this simple practice as a way to foster trust within your team. Do this at every meeting, and you may find your team members gradually gravitating toward mutual trust.

Empathic Listening

If you have been practicing Mindful Conversation (the looping and dipping thing from Chapter 3), you may by now be skilled at listening mindfully and enjoying admiration from your peers for your listening prowess. It is time to go one up from here, Grasshopper. Let us now up-skill ourselves from mindful listening to empathic listening, and become able to listen for feelings.

Empathic listening is a very powerful skill. During one empathic listening exercise in Search Inside Yourself, I played the role of a participant to fill a vacancy. As part of the exercise, I listened for my exercise partner's feelings as she spoke, and then I told her what I thought she felt. After I was done, she started to cry. I asked her what happened, and she said she had not felt this understood in a very long time. That was when I realized the power of empathic listening. People thirst for others to understand their feelings, and when somebody does, it touches them so deeply that they sometimes cry. Imagine how much good you can do for people if you are skillful at listening empathically.

In Search Inside Yourself, we practice empathic listening as a formal Mindful Conversation exercise (from Chapter 3) with one important change. In Mindful Conversation, the listener doing the looping begins her feedback with "What I hear you say is . . ." In this exercise, the listener doing the looping will begin her feedback with "What I hear you *feel* is . . ." This requires the listener to listen for feelings and then to give feedback about feelings.

FORMAL PRACTICE OF EMPATHIC LISTENING

This is a Mindful Conversation exercise (see Chapter 3), but instead of listening for content, you listen for feelings.

Get in pairs and take turns being the speaker and the listener. As usual, the speaker begins with a monologue. If you are the listener, after the speaker's monologue, you loop about what you heard the speaker was feeling. In other words, instead of starting your looping with, "What I hear you say is . . ." start with, "What I hear you *feel* is . . ."

Suggested topics for monologue:

- A difficult work situation or a conflict you are having with a boss, co-worker, or person who reports to you
- A time when you could feel someone else's pain, or when you wanted to but were unable to
- Any other topic with emotional "juice"

(continued)

Meta-Conversation

After each of you has taken your turn being the speaker and listener, have a meta-conversation about how the conversations went.

In class, after we complete this exercise, we deliver the punch line: We never explain to the class *how* to do empathic listening. We assume people already know how.

And it works. Usually, after we deliver the punch line, folks in the class become pleasantly surprised by how well they listened empathically without any instruction. They discover for themselves that empathic listening is an ability we are born with; it is part of the standard package that comes installed as part of our social brain. The only thing we have to do is improve it with practice.

Specifically, there are four things we can do to strengthen our ability for empathic listening.

1. Mindfulness: With mindfulness, we become more perceptive and receptive.
2. Kindness: When we are kind, we can listen better to feelings.
3. Curiosity: Practice wondering what someone might be feeling when you hear their stories.
4. Practice: Just do a lot of empathic listening. The more you do it, the better you become, especially when you practice it in conjunction with mindfulness, kindness, and curiosity.

Given those insights, below are some suggestions for how you can practice empathic listening informally in an everyday setting. Note that the informal practice is a little trickier than the formal practice. In formal practice, we get to create an artificial environment to talk about how well we are listening to each other's feelings, but in natural conversation, we do not usually say, "I'm going to tell you what I heard you feel, and you let me know how well I'm doing, yeah?" That is a little awkward. Hence, for the informal practice, I suggest that you focus more on your own inner qualities involved in empathic listening, tread lightly in giving feedback, and feel free to stay close to your own comfort zone. Remember that people generally do not like to be told how they feel, even if you are right (you can try this one at home if you need confirmation: "Clearly you're feeling hurt." "I am not!"). So, ask about feelings, or at least remember to start with "This is what I hear" and give the speaker a chance to correct you if you haven't got it exactly right. Your empathic listening will get better with practice, even if you stay well within your own comfort zone, as long as you put mindfulness, kindness, and curiosity into your effort every time.

INFORMAL PRACTICE OF EMPATHIC LISTENING

Preparing for the Conversation

The qualities that are most conducive to empathic listening are mindfulness and kindness. If you have time to prepare for the conversation, prime the pump for these qualities, first with a few minutes of Mindfulness Meditation (see Chapter 2). When your mind is in that mindful state, you will be more able to pay attention to feelings, both your own and the other person's. You will also be more able to listen without judging, which allows you to become more open to what you will hear. If you have more time, do a few minutes of the Just Like Me / Loving Kindness exercise from earlier in this chapter toward the other person. Putting yourself in this frame of mind makes the other person more receptive to you, and you more receptive to him or her.

(continued)

During the Conversation

Begin the conversation by thinking to yourself, "I want this person to be happy." When listening, practice Mindful Listening (see Chapter 3). Remind yourself to listen for the other person's feelings. Be curious about what he or she may be feeling. Give him or her generous amounts of airtime.

If it is appropriate for the situation and you are comfortable doing so, you may ask the other person how he or she is feeling. If the situation warrants it and you are comfortable doing so, you may tell him or her (gently and with kindness), "I hear that you are feeling . . ." Generously allow him or her to respond. If you are right about what he or she felt, he or she may feel touched that you understood and may let you know. If you are wrong, allow him or her to tell you so, and listen in a kind and open manner.

Meta-Conversation

If it is appropriate for the situation and you are comfortable doing so, at the end of the conversation, you may initiate a meta-conversation by asking, "Was this conversation helpful to you?"

Praising People Skillfully

Besides listening to people empathically, something else you can do to bring out their best is to praise them. First and foremost, always praise authentically (or, never praise falsely)—if your praise is not genuine, it will be sniffed out and you will lose credibility. However, even when your praises are genuine, you need to learn to praise skillfully. It turns out that you can undermine people by praising them, even when you are doing it with the best of intentions!

In studies by Claudia Mueller and Carol Dweck, fifth-grade students were given a problem-solving task engineered to guarantee high performance, and the students were praised for their success.[11] Some students were praised for their intelligence ("person praise": "You must be smart at these problems"), some were praised for their effort ("process praise": "You must have worked hard at these problems"), and the remaining students, the control group, were simply told their scores were very high. Later, on a subsequent set of harder problems, those praised for being smart performed significantly worse than the other groups, while those praised for their effort significantly outperformed the other groups. Being praised for being smart is bad for you.

The explanation offered by researchers in these and related studies is that when a person is given person praise, it reinforces a "fixed mind-set," or the belief that our success is due to fixed traits that are a given. People in this mind-set worry about their traits. They also worry about how adequate or inadequate they might be. When they fail, they attribute it to personal inadequacy. They are afraid to take risks when failure may show them to be inadequate. In contrast, when a person is given process praise, it reinforces a "growth mind-set," or the belief that our qualities can be developed through dedication and effort, and therefore that success comes from dedication and effort. This creates a love of learning and resilience that is essential for great accomplishment.[12]

Thus, when giving feedback, it is best to do so in a way that encourages a growth mind-set. It is better to structure feedback around effort and growth than by labeling the person.

Simply put, it's better to praise people for working hard than for being smart. Oh, and thank you for reading this book. You must have worked hard at it. Good effort!

Political Awareness Is Empathy++

Now that we have learned empathy skills for one-on-one interactions, it is time to up our game to a more difficult skill: the ability to read an organization's emotional currents and power relationships. The common name for this skill is "political awareness."

Political awareness is one of the most useful skills you can equip yourself with in any organization. Happily, this skill is not foreign to a practitioner of empathy because, in a sense, political awareness is the generalization of empathy from an interpersonal level to an organizational level. Daniel Goleman describes it this way:

Every organization has its own invisible nervous system of connection and influence. . . . Some people are oblivious to this below-the-radar world, while others have it fully on their own screen. Skill at reading the currents that influence the real decision-makers depends on the ability to empathize on an organizational level, not just an interpersonal one.[13]

Another way to look at it—in "plain vanilla" empathy—you understand the feelings, needs, and concerns of individual people. In political awareness, you understand the feelings, needs, and concerns of individual people *and* how those feelings, needs, and concerns interact with those of others and how that all weaves into the emotional fabric of the organization as a whole. There are a lot more variables to understand in political awareness, but the basic skill required is the same.

If you understand people and you understand the interactions between them, you will understand the whole organization. That is political awareness.

Practices for Political Awareness

On top of the (plain vanilla) empathy practices already mentioned in this chapter, there are other useful practices for developing political awareness. My wise friend Marc Lesser recommends the practices below based on his many years of experience being a CEO and executive coach.

1. Maintain rich personal networks within your organization, especially with allies, mentors, and groups who will support and challenge you. To do this, care about people, help people, and nurture relationships. Pay attention to one-on-one relationships, as well as relationships with key groups—your team, other management teams, customers, stakeholders, etc.

2. Practice reading the underlying currents of your organization. Understand how decisions are made. Are decisions made by authority or consensus? Who are most influential in making them?

3. Distinguish between your own self-interest, the interest of your team, and the organization's interest—everyone has all three of these interests. It is very important to understand which is which.

4. Utilize your self-awareness to better understand your role in the web of personalities and interactions. Make frequent use of empathic listening to understand how people feel about situations and about each other.

Here is an exercise to help you increase political awareness.

POLITICAL AWARENESS EXERCISE

You may do this as either a writing exercise or a speaking exercise. If you do this as a speaking exercise, you may speak to a friend.

Instructions

1. Think of a difficult situation from your present or past, when there was some conflict or disagreement, something real, something that has some meaning and potency for you.
2. Describe the situation as though you are 100 percent correct and reasonable. Do that either in writing or by talking about it in a monologue.
3. Now describe the situation as though the other person is (or the other people are) 100 percent correct and reasonable. Do that either in writing or by talking about it in a monologue.

If you did this as a speaking exercise with a friend, discuss the contents of your monologues in a free-flow conversation.

The main purpose of this exercise is to practice seeing the perspectives of different players (in this case, yourself and another party) objectively. You may notice that the instructions were worded very carefully. The key learning point (that is, the kicker) is the insight that the stories in steps two and three can very often be precisely the same story. In other words, conflict does not always arise because one side is wrong or unreasonable. It is entirely possible for both sides to be 100 percent correct and 100 percent reasonable and still have conflict.

There are many reasons why this can happen. One common reason is that people implicitly value different priorities. For example, one engineer might place higher priority on meeting the delivery schedule, as she might think it is better to deliver a promised product on time even if it means cutting down the number of features. Another engineer might place higher priority on completeness of delivery, as he might think it is better to give the customer everything he was promised the first time, even if it means delivering late. In this case, they may each be correct and reasonable, and still they may get into an unending disagreement, unless each is able to understand and internalize the other's implicit priorities.

Another common reason is that we have incomplete data, which happens a lot in real life, and we all have our own reasonable ways of filling in the missing pieces. For example, let's say we are presented with a large business opportunity that can easily double or triple our revenue in a few years, but it requires us to make a large investment that exceeds our current net assets. Is this opportunity so compelling we have to do it, or is it so risky it will bankrupt us? Nobody can possibly know for sure, because nobody can know in advance how many new customers it will actually bring in each year. We can only give our best guess. In such situations, it is possible to have huge disagreements in which both sides are correct and reasonable. These disagreements will remain unresolved until people assume that the other is reasonable and become open to each other's implicit assumptions.

The more often you are able to see how each side in a disagreement is correct and reasonable, the more often you will be able to understand differing perspectives objectively and the more accurate your political awareness will become.

This reminds me of a joke: Two guys had a major disagreement they could not resolve, so they decided to consult a wise guru. The first guy presented his argument to the guru, and the guru nodded his head and said, "Yes, you are right." The second guy presented his diametrically opposing argument to the guru, and again the guru nodded his head and said, "Yes, you are right."

A third guy watching the entire exchange got a little bit annoyed and asked the guru, "Wait, something is wrong. They cannot possibly both be right at the same time." And the guru nodded his head and said, "Yes, you are right."

Mental Habits for Highly Empathetic People

Empathy comes preinstalled in our brains; we are all hardwired to be empathic. However, the main takeaway of this chapter is that empathy is something you can improve with practice, and most of that practice involves mindfulness and creating mental habits that are conducive to empathy.

Chief among those mental habits is kindness. Having the mental habit of kindness means that every time you interact with a human being, the thoughts in your mind that arise habitually and effortlessly are, "This person is a human being just like me. I want him or her to be happy." Having this mental habit makes you more receptive to other people, and them more receptive to you.

Another mental habit is being open to understanding how other people can seem reasonable, at least from their own points of view, even when you disagree with them. Having this mental habit enables you to view social interactions with more clarity and objectivity.

If you practice mindfulness frequently and foster the above mental habits, you will have a very strong foundation for empathy. If, on top of that foundation, you also practice a lot of empathic listening and pay frequent attention to people, you will eventually develop strong empathy that extends to political awareness.

And that is no monkey business.

CHAPTER EIGHT

Being Effective and Loved at the Same Time

Leadership and Social Skills

You can make more friends in two months by becoming really interested in other people than you can in two years by trying to get other people interested in you. Which is just another way of saying that the way to make a friend is to be one.

—Dale Carnegie

Being Loved Is Good for Your Career

Two renowned leadership scholars, Jim Kouzes and Barry Posner, offer the following research conclusion:

> *. . . researchers looked at a number of factors that could account for a manager's success. [They] found one, and only one, factor significantly differentiated the top quartile of managers from the bottom quartile*

> *. . . the single factor was high scores on* **affection***—both expressed and wanted . . . the highest performing managers show more warmth and fondness toward others than do the bottom 25 percent. They get closer to people, and they are significantly more open in sharing thoughts and feelings than their low-performing counterparts.*
>
> *. . . All things being equal, we will work harder and more effectively for people we like. And we like them in direct proportion to how they make us feel.*[1]

To those of us in the corporate world used to the idea that the most effective way to get things done is to act like a jerk, this study offers a refreshing and inspiring possibility of a better approach. You do not necessarily have to get things done at the expense of being liked; it is possible to have both. You can have your cake and promotion too. In fact, being liked may be the most effective way to get things done in the long term. This possibility is also reflected in the study of U.S. Navy commanders we quoted in Chapter 1, which showed that the most effective naval commanders are also the ones with higher emotional intelligence and who are most liked.

"You know, Lord Vader, you'd be much more effective if you were more likable."

In this chapter, we will explore some emotional skills that will help you be liked and also be successful at what you do. Some people buy books that teach them to be liked, others buy books that teach them to be successful. This book teaches you both. You are so lucky.

Using Kindness to Grow Friendship from an Ugly Situation

Even in difficult situations, it is sometimes possible to make important things happen while still creating happy friendships. It requires a kind heart, an open mind, and the right social skills.

Many years ago, I had a friend and co-worker named Joe (names have been changed, again to protect me). Joe was never on my team, but his work involved building systems used internally in the company, so in that sense, I was Joe's customer and a very satisfied one. A new manager, Sam, joined the company and took over Joe's team, and within a few weeks, Sam called Joe into his office and told him his performance had been very unsatisfactory and dismissal procedures would soon be initiated against him.

Joe was devastated. I was very unhappy too. As a customer of the team, I considered Joe one of its best performers, so I was angry that Joe would even be evaluated poorly, let alone dismissed on performance grounds. I was determined to help him.

I was an influential person in that company, so if I had confronted Joe's new manager, Sam, the potential for things to become really ugly was obvious, even to an engineer like me.

Fortunately, I already had years of meditation and compassion practice, so I had the right tools to deal skillfully with this situation. I calmed my mind with mindfulness and used the Just Like Me meditation (see Chapter 7) to put myself into Sam's shoes. I quickly realized that there must be something important I did not know about the situation and which I needed to understand before I judged. I was missing important data. My mind quickly shifted from anger to an eagerness to understand and engage with kindness and curiosity.

I wrote Sam an e-mail introducing myself, sincerely welcoming him to the company, and then explained my concerns about Joe and my eagerness to help him. Part of the e-mail read:

> *I understand that we are all reasonable people, so that decision must not have been made lightly. However, I hope to be able to understand the reasons behind that decision, so that I can figure out how to better help Joe.*
>
> *Will you be comfortable if I schedule some time with you so that I can listen to and learn from you about this case? I don't want to put you in an uncomfortable position, so please feel free to say no.*

Happily, Sam, though understandably a bit uncomfortable, engaged me with reciprocal kindness and sincerity. We sat together, exchanged personal stories, and then talked about Joe. We both learned a lot in that conversation. From Sam, I learned that Joe had created issues for his team, such as taking on too much from his customers in an undisciplined manner that caused him to neglect some important team goals. On the other end, Sam learned from me how much Joe's customers valued him for all those extra miles he had gone for them. Sam and I both acquired important missing data.

Soon after that, Sam and Joe talked again, established a better understanding of each other, and figured out how they can work effectively together. Dismissal proceedings against Joe were dropped. Sam and I established a great friendship that is still strong to this day.

What could have been an ugly drama instead became the starting point of a long friendship. This is the usefulness of emotional skills used in a social setting.

There is an old Chinese Zen saying: "The small [meditation] retreat is in the wilderness, the medium retreat is in the city, and the great retreat is in the emperor's court." Like most Zen sayings, this one is both absurd and true. All the emotional skills you learn in this book are useless if they cannot be applied in the real world, including a setting as seductive and dangerous as the emperor's court. Conversely, the real world is the best place to sharpen your emotional skills. The real world is both your dojo and your zendo, from which you will get your mojo. Yo?

In this chapter, we will learn three essential social skills: leading with compassion, influencing with goodness, and communicating with insight.

Leading with Compassion

Compassion is known in every faith tradition and numerous philosophies as a great virtue. It is not just a great virtue, however. Compassion is also the cause for the highest level of happiness ever measured, and it's a necessary condition for the most effective form of leadership known. Amazing stuff.

Compassion Is the Happiest State

Earlier in this book, we talked (and joked) about my friend Matthieu Ricard, the "happiest man in the world." When Matthieu's brain was scanned and measured with fMRI, his measure of happiness was extremely high. He was actually not the only person to register that extreme level of happiness—a number of Tibetan Buddhist meditation masters (people we consider the "Olympians" of the meditation world) were measured in the same lab, and more than one registered extreme levels of happiness. Matthieu was the first subject whose identity was unintentionally leaked to the public, which earned him that nickname. Another subject whose identity recently became known is Mingyur Rinpoche. Mingyur is similarly nicknamed in the Chinese-language press as the "happiest person in the world."

These folks are, by far, the happiest people ever measured by science. Which leads us to a question: what were they thinking when they were being measured? Something naughty, perhaps? There is something about monks and their monk-y business, you know. Actually, they were meditating on compassion. This must be mind-blowing to many people because many of us consider compassion to be an unpleasant mental state, but here is scientific data showing precisely the reverse—that compassion is a state of extreme happiness.

I asked Matthieu about it. His own first-person experience confirms the data. In his experience, *compassion is the happiest state ever.* Being the engineer I am, I asked him the most obvious follow-up question, what is the second happiest state ever? He said, "Open awareness," a state in which the mind is extremely open, calm, and clear. I don't know about you, but as a practicing meditator, I found that insight stunning. As meditators, we train the mind toward profound calmness and clarity. As our practice deepens, we become increasingly happy, and since this deepening happiness does not require sensual or mental stimulation, some of us fall into the danger of withdrawing from real life (as usual, the Zen folks have the funniest description; they call them "Zen bums"). It turns out that even when you perfect that practice, the most you can achieve is the second happiest state.

The happiest state can only be achieved with compassion, which requires engagement in real life with real people. Hence, our meditation practices cannot be perfected outside of real life; there has to be a combination of seclusion from the world (to deepen the calmness) and engagement with the world (to deepen the compassion). If you are a deep meditator, remember to open your door and go out once in a while.

When I first read about these studies done on Matthieu (which was before we knew each other in person), it became one of the pivotal moments of my life. My dream is to create the conditions for world peace, and to do that by creating the conditions for inner peace and compassion on a global scale. Learning about Matthieu gave me a new angle for looking at my work. The insight that compassion can be fun changes the entire game. If compassion is a chore, nobody will do it, except maybe the Dalai Lama. But if compassion is fun, everybody is going to do it. Therefore, to create the conditions for global compassion, all we have to do is reframe compassion as something that is fun. Wow. Who knew saving the world would require fun?

Happily, compassion is not just fun. It has very real business benefits as well, especially in the context of business leadership.

Compassionate Leadership Is the Most Effective Leadership

The best definition of compassion I know comes from the eminent Tibetan scholar Thupten Jinpa. Jinpa is also the longtime English translator for the Dalai Lama. He has a charmingly mellow and gentle voice, so the Dalai Lama mischievously makes gentle fun of it every now and then ("See, I have deep booming voice, but this guy, his voice so soft," the Dalai Lama would say, and they would all laugh out loud).

Jinpa defines compassion as follows:

> *Compassion is a mental state endowed with a sense of concern for the suffering of others and aspiration to see that suffering relieved.*

Specifically, he defines compassion as having three components:

1. A cognitive component: "I understand you"
2. An affective component: "I feel for you"
3. A motivational component: "I want to help you"

The most compelling benefit of compassion in the context of work is that compassion creates highly effective leaders. To become a highly effective leader, you need to go through an important transformation. Bill George, the widely respected former CEO of Medtronic puts it most succinctly, calling it going from "I" to "We."

> *This shift is the transformation from "I" to "We." It is the most important process leaders go through in becoming authentic. How else*

> *can they unleash the power of their organizations unless they motivate people to reach their full potential? If our supporters are merely following our lead, then their efforts are limited to our vision and our directions. . . . Only when leaders stop focusing on their personal ego needs are they able to develop other leaders.*[2]

The practice of compassion is about going from self to others. In a way, compassion is about going from "I" to "We." So if switching from "I" to "We" is the most important process of becoming an authentic leader, those who practice compassion will already know how and will have a head start.

But wait, there's more. I found the work of Jim Collins, documented in his book *Good to Great: Why Some Companies Make the Leap . . . and Others Don't,*[3] to be even more illuminating. I tell all my friends that if they only read one business book in their entire lives, the one to read is *Good to Great.* The premise of the book is itself fascinating: Collins and his team tried to discover what makes companies go from good to great by sifting through a massive amount of data. They started with the set of every company that has appeared on Fortune 500 from 1965 to 1995, and they identified companies that started out merely as "good" companies that then became "great" companies (defined as outperforming the general market by a factor of three or more) for an extended period of time (defined as fifteen years or more, to weed out the one-hit wonders and those that were merely lucky). They ended up with a set of eleven "good to great" companies and compared them to a set of "comparison companies" to determine what made the merely good companies become great.

Being a data-loving Google engineer, I find the premise of the book and its heavy reliance on data fascinating. I find equally fascinating how well its findings seem to work in real life. Many of the principles from the book felt remarkably similar to what I experienced at Google in its early years. A casual observer who has read *Good to Great* and who is also familiar with Google's history might mistakenly think all of us early employees at

Google knew the book by heart. So, if you want to found the next Google, I recommend you read *Good to Great.*

The first and perhaps the most important finding in the book is the role of leadership. It takes a very special type of leader to bring a company from goodness to greatness. Collins calls them "Level 5" leaders. These are leaders who, in addition to being highly capable, also possess a paradoxical mix of two important and seemingly conflicting qualities: great ambition and personal humility. These leaders are highly ambitious, but the focus of their ambition is not themselves; instead, they are ambitious for the greater good. Because their attention is focused on the greater good, they feel no need to inflate their own egos. That makes them highly effective and inspiring.

"I said great ambition and personal *humility.*"

While Collins's book convincingly demonstrates the importance of Level 5 leaders, it (understandably) does not prescribe a way to train them. I do not pretend to know how to train Level 5 leaders either, but I am convinced that compassion plays an essential role.

If you look at the two distinguishing qualities of Level 5 leaders (ambition and personal humility) in the context of the three components of compassion (cognitive, affective, motivational), you may find that the cognitive and affective components of compassion (understanding people and empathizing with them) tone down the excessive self-obsession within us, and thereby create the conditions for humility. The motivational component of compassion, wanting to help people, creates ambition for greater good. In other words, the three components of compassion can be used to train the two distinguishing qualities of Level 5 leadership.

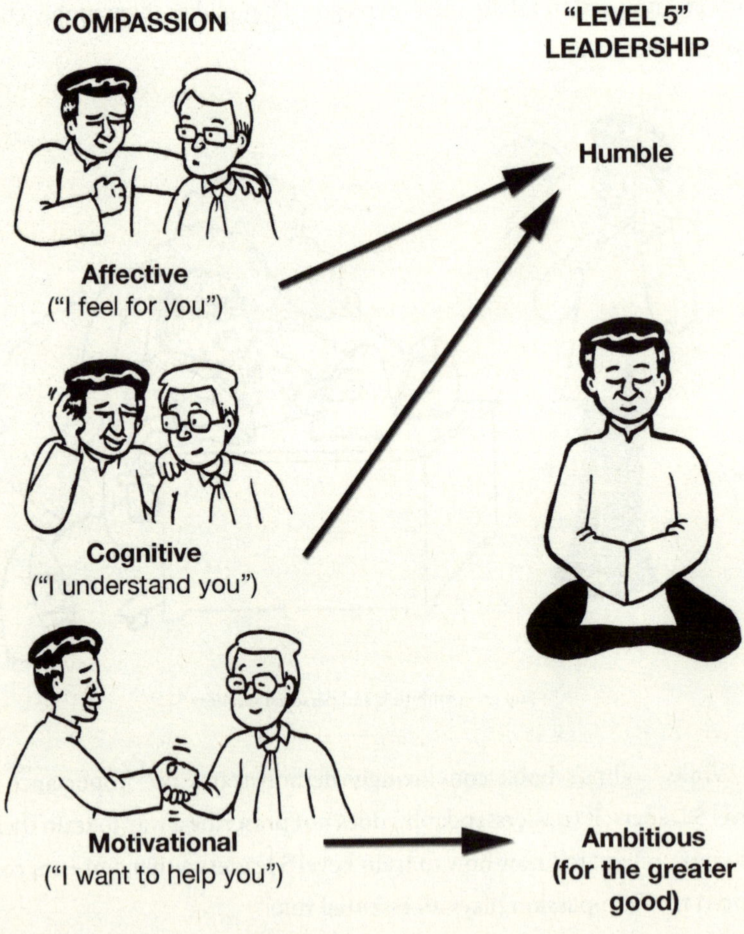

Compassion is a necessary (but maybe insufficient) condition for Level 5 leadership, and therefore, one way to begin training Level 5 leaders is compassion training. This is one compelling benefit of compassion at work.

Training Compassion by Multiplying Goodness

We can train compassion similar to the way we train loving kindness, by creating mental habits. The premise is the same: the more you think about something, the stronger the neural pathways conducive to that thought become, and the easier it is to have that thought. Eventually, that thought becomes a mental habit and arises frequently and effortlessly. The mental habit that we are going to use for training compassion is something powerful yet pleasant at the same time: goodness. We increase the ability of the mind to perceive and increase goodness, both within ourselves and toward others.

For this practice, we'll also employ another powerful mental tool: visualization. Our brains devote a substantial amount of resources to processing visual perception, so in theory, if we can make skillful use of the visual perception system for any mental task, we can take advantage of a lot more of the brain's computational resources. In practice, I find that if I can visualize something, I can make it stick better. So, in this meditation, we will use visualization as a way of increasing the effectiveness of creating the mental habits for compassion.

The practice itself is very simple. When we breathe in, we visualize that we're breathing in our own goodness, we visualize multiplying that goodness by ten in our hearts, and then when we breathe out, we visualize giving all that goodness to the world. After that, we breathe in the goodness of other people and do the same. If you want, you may visualize the goodness as white light.

Try doing this at home.

MULTIPLYING GOODNESS MEDITATION

Resting the Mind

Start with 2 minutes of resting the mind on the breath.

Multiplying Goodness

Now, let us connect with the goodness within ourselves: our love, compassion, altruism, and inner joy. If you wish, you may visualize your goodness radiating out of your body as a faint white light.

(Short pause)

When you breathe in, breathe all your goodness into your heart. Use your heart to multiply that goodness by a factor of ten. And when you breathe out, send all that goodness out to the whole world. If you wish, you may visualize yourself breathing out a brilliant white light representing this abundance of goodness.

(2-minute pause)

Now, let us connect with the goodness within everybody we know. Everybody we know is a good person, possessing some goodness. If you wish, you may visualize their goodness radiating out of their bodies as a faint white light. When you breathe in, breathe all their goodness into your heart . . . (Repeat above.)

(2-minute pause)

Finally, let us connect with the goodness within everybody in the world. Everybody in the world possesses at least a hint of goodness. If you wish, you may visualize their goodness radiating out of their bodies as a faint white light. When you breathe in, breathe all their goodness into your heart . . . (Repeat above.)

(2-minute pause)

Closing

End with a 1-minute rest of the mind on the breath.

This practice develops three useful mental habits:

1. Seeing goodness in self and others
2. Giving goodness to all
3. Confidence in the transformative power of self (that I can multiply goodness)

The first habit (seeing goodness) strengthens the affective and cognitive components of compassion. When you instinctively and habitually perceive goodness in everyone, you instinctively want to understand and feel for them. Even in difficult situations, instead of simply dismissing the other person as a jerk and walking away, you want to understand that person because there is at least a hint of goodness in him that you can see. If you do this a lot, eventually, you become one whom people trust because you understand and care.

The next habit (giving goodness) strengthens the motivational component of compassion. When you instinctively and habitually want to deliver goodness to the world, pretty soon, you become the person who always wants to help others. Eventually, you become one whom people respect, sometimes even admire, because they feel your heart is in the right place.

The last habit (confidence in the transformative power of self) strengthens self-confidence. When you become comfortable with the idea that your heart can multiply goodness by a factor of ten, your emotional brain soon becomes comfortable with the idea that "Yes, I can benefit people." Eventually, you may become one who inspires. And then maybe you will become a Level 5 leader.

"I want to deliver goodness to the world, but the world keeps requesting crap."

Compassion Training for the Brave

The traditional practice for developing compassion is something known as *Tonglen*, which in Tibetan means "giving and receiving." It is a lot like the Multiplying Goodness practice, except instead of breathing in goodness, you breathe in suffering (of self and others), and transform it within yourself. When you breathe out, you radiate love, kindness, and compassion.

This practice turns out to be very hard for novice meditators because it requires you to breathe in and receive pain and suffering. You do not have to do this, but if you are brave enough, please feel free to try it out. Here are instructions you can use:

TONGLEN MEDITATION

Pre-Meditation Script

In order to master social skills, we have to clear out the emotional gunk—anger, fear, confusion, and even physical suffering, and our resistance to it all. Tonglen is a practice designed for this effect, centered on awareness of breathing.

Tonglen literally means "giving and receiving," willingness to receive the suffering and pain of others, and giving relief, well-being, and peace in return—thereby experiencing our ability to be transformers.

By breathing in negativity, we can use the heart as a filter. Breathing out, the dark clouds can pass through us, and transform into acceptance, ease, joy, and light/radiance. When we experience this, we strengthen the resolve that nothing can totally overcome us, which establishes deep confidence. This gives us a strong foothold to stand up for the well-being of ourselves and others, thereby building the foundation for compassion.

Settling In

Let's begin by becoming aware of our bodies and our breathing, noting sensations all through the body and gently focusing attention on the ebb and flow of the breath.

(Pause)

Now take a deep breath and imagine on the out breath that you feel you are a mountain.

Take another deep breath and imagine you are viewing life with an elevated perspective.

(continued)

Tonglen

And with another breath, let's start Tonglen practice, by beginning with ourselves.

With the generosity of an open heart and mind, imagine you can see yourself sitting in front of you. Look at your "ordinary self," with its suffering—whatever might be troubling you lately.

Breathe this in as if it is a dark cloud of gunk, and let it disperse and transform.

Breathe it out as rays of light. Repeat this breathing cycle for a short time.

(Pause)

Notice if you feel more tenderness, understanding, and warmth for yourself.

(Pause)

Now let's practice for others:

Imagine you see in front of you someone in your life who is suffering.

With an in breath, feel how open you can be to his or her experience. Perhaps you can feel a strong intention arising to relieve this person of his or her difficulties.

Breathe this in as a dark cloud and feel it entering your heart, where it dissolves any traces of self-interest to reveal your innate goodness.

Breathe out rays of light, setting your intention to alleviate suffering.

Let's spend some time breathing in and out like this.

(Pause)

Closing

For the last few moments, you can bring your hand to your chest and just breathe.

Tonglen is a very powerful practice. The Dalai Lama is said to do this every day as one of his main practices. The first time I did this practice (under the guidance of Zen master Norman Fischer; the script above came from him), I experienced profound change. In those few minutes, I experienced a permanent strengthening of my self-confidence. I realized during the practice that a lot of what was holding me back originated from my fear of pain and suffering, and once I found myself capable of breathing in the pain and suffering of myself and others, and comfortable radiating kindness, love, and compassion, a lot of the fetters holding me back dissolved away.

"There've been complaints about who you've gotten to help breathe in your pain and suffering . . ."

We taught Tonglen during the early iterations of Search Inside Yourself, but we soon discovered it to be too hard for many participants. The near-consensus among Search Inside Yourself instructors was to take it out of the curriculum, but I strongly dissented. Tonglen is such a powerful and useful practice, I insisted that we needed to keep it. We eventually came up with a great solution that addressed everybody's concerns by creating the Multiplying Goodness practice, which is useful and easy for novices to pick up, and it also allows a sneak preview into Tonglen. That is why you will likely not see that Multiplying Goodness practice described as a traditional practice for another hundred years or so, by which time I will be quite old, I think.

My suggestion to you is to start by practicing Multiplying Goodness, and once you feel more confident in your own practice (perhaps after a few weeks), give Tonglen a try. It may change you in profound ways.

Influencing with Goodness

The first rule of influence is that we all already have it. Everything we do or don't do, and everything we say or don't say, has an effect on other people. The key is not to acquire influence, but to expand the influence we already have and to use it for the good of all.

Understanding the Social Brain

I find that the most important first step to expanding our influence is to understand the social brain well enough to skillfully navigate it.

According to neuroscientist Evian Gordon, the "minimize danger and maximize reward" principle is an overarching, organizing principle of the brain. The brain is a machine that primarily approaches reward and avoids threat, as illustrated in the diagram below.

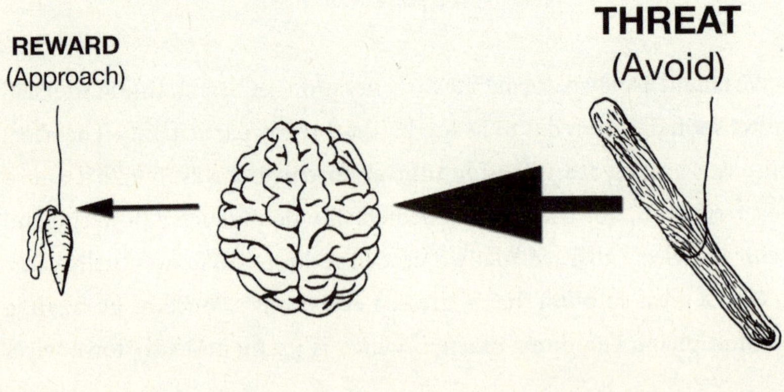

Notice that the "Reward (Approach)" arrow is much smaller than the "Threat (Avoid)" arrow. The difference in size illustrates the important insight that our brains respond far more strongly to negative experiences than comparable positive ones. We all experience this every day. For example, if I walk past Jim in the hallway and smile at him and he smiles back, it's a very minor positive social experience for me and it affects me only very slightly. Most likely, the experience would fade out of my mind in a few moments. However, let's say Jim does not smile back, he just looks away slightly grim-faced and continues walking. Objectively, it's roughly comparable in magnitude (in the negative direction) to him smiling back at me, but subjectively, I am likely to react much more strongly. I might go, "*Whoa,* what's up with that? What's wrong with that guy? What did I do to him this time?" Instead of a few moments, this one might last many minutes, perhaps even longer. Negative experiences impact us more strongly and last much longer than positive ones do.

How many positive experiences does it take to balance out a comparable negative experience? It depends on who you ask. In Chapter 6, we mentioned the groundbreaking work of psychologist Barbara Fredrickson, which suggests the ratio to be 3:1. She discovered that "experiencing positive emotions in a 3-to-1 ratio with negative ones leads people to a tipping point beyond which they naturally become more resilient to adversity and effortlessly achieve what they once could only imagine."[4] Famed psychologist John Gottman, however, found a different ratio in a different context. He found that for a marriage to succeed, there must be at least five times as many positive interactions in the relationship as negative ones, a 5:1 ratio that Gottman dubbed the "magic ratio,"[5] more commonly known as the "Gottman ratio." This ratio is such a powerful predictor that Gottman reputedly can accurately predict if a marriage will end in divorce within ten years just by scoring the positive and negative interactions in a fifteen-minute conversation between the couple. He jokes that this is why he does not get invited to dinner parties anymore.

If you put these two ratios together side by side, you immediately understand why marriage is so tough. We demand an unreasonable 3:1

positivity ratio for all our daily experiences, except in our marriage, from which we demand even more. In that sense, we all behave like over-demanding jerks toward our spouses, and we judge them far more harshly than we judge mere acquaintances. Maybe if we understand that, we could give our spouses a little bit of a well-deserved break, and maybe marriage would not be quite so tough.

The SCARF Model for the Social Brain

In *Your Brain at Work,* David Rock describes five domains of social experience that the brain treats as primary rewards or threats. In other words, these five domains are so important to you that your brain treats them in the same way it treats survival issues. And because they are so important, each is a major driver of social behavior. These five domains form a model which David calls the SCARF model, which stands for Status, Certainty, Autonomy, Relatedness, and Fairness.[6]

Status

Status is about relative importance, pecking order, or seniority. People go to great lengths to protect or increase their status. Status is so important, it even predicts longevity, both in humans and in primates. Status threats can also be triggered very easily. For example, just talking to your boss can activate a status threat. When a co-worker asks to give you "feedback," that too can trigger a status threat.

The good news is there is a good way to increase your own status without harming others, and that is what David calls "playing against yourself." When you improve a skill (such as improving your golf handicap), you activate a status reward relative to your former self. This is perhaps why mastery is such a powerful motivator (see Chapter 6). When you gain increasing mastery over something that matters to you, you activate a status reward, at least when compared against your former self.

Certainty

Our brains love certainty. Uncertainty generates "error responses" in the brain that cannot be ignored until they are resolved. In other words, uncertainty takes away valuable brain resources. Larger uncertainties can be highly debilitating. For example, if you do not know whether your job is secure, uncertainty will probably occupy most of your mind and you may not be able to do much else at work.

Autonomy

Autonomy is the perception of exerting control over one's environment. According to Steve Maier, "the degree of control that organisms can exert over something that creates stress determines whether the stressor alters the organism's functioning."[7] In other words, it's not the stress itself that gets to you; it's the feeling of helplessness in the face of that stress. There are many studies that give strong evidence to this. One study, for example, shows that low-level British civil servants have more stress-related health problems than senior executives, even though the latter are known to be under a lot more stress.

Relatedness

Relatedness is the perception of whether another person is a "friend" or a "foe." It makes sense for relatedness to be part of our primary reward/threat circuitry, since our very survival used to be almost entirely dependent on other people in our own tightly cooperating small tribes. In fact, relatedness is so fundamental, some research shows that the one and only experience in life that makes people sustainably happy over time is the quality and quantity of social connections. (They did not study accomplished meditators, so while I agree with that finding, I suspect there is a little bit more to that story.) Warren Buffett, one of the richest men in the world, demonstrated that he understood the power of relatedness when he said, "When you get to my age, you'll measure your success in life by how many of the people you want to have love you actually do love you. That's the ultimate test of how you've lived your life."

By default, the brain labels someone a foe unless proven otherwise. For example, strangers are usually labeled as foe (or at least, labeled as "approach at your own risk"). Fortunately, in many situations, it is not hard to switch people from foes to friends. For example, all it usually takes is a handshake and a pleasant conversation. Many practices in this book, such as Just Like Me and Loving Kindness can greatly ease and accelerate this process.

Fairness

Humans are the only animals known to voluntarily injure their own self-interests to punish the perceived unfairness of others. Other primates are known to punish unfairness, but not at the expense of their own self-interest. For example, say we are in a game (known as the Ultimatum Game) in which person A (the "proposer") is given one hundred dollars, which he must distribute between himself and person B (the "responder"). If person B accepts the deal, they both pocket the money as distributed by A, but if B rejects the deal, they both go home empty-handed. If person A distributes ninety-nine dollars to himself and one dollar to B, objectively, B has no reason to reject the deal. If B accepts the deal, he gets a dollar, and if he rejects it, he gets nothing. There is only one economically rational course of action for him. Yet many people in the position of person B will reject the deal out of being offended by unfairness. In contrast, a chimpanzee playing a similar game (using raisins as the object of value rather than U.S. dollars) will rarely reject that deal.[8] To a chimp, forgoing raisins is just silly. The moral of the story is to never underestimate a person's sense of fairness; it is overwhelming enough that he often may sacrifice his own self-interest for its sake. (The other moral of the story is to never count on a chimpanzee giving you a fair deal. Nor an elephant, for that matter.)

"With Judge Bonzo presiding, we might have to revisit our initial projections about the success of your case."

Expanding Your Influence

You can influence people most effectively when you help people achieve what they want in a way that also helps you and simultaneously serves greater good. That is why the SCARF model from the previous section can be so valuable. By understanding the neuroscience of the social brain, you can better understand how your actions can increase the SCARF factors for self and others, hence you can figure out how to help people in ways that also align with your own interests. For example, if you take the time to know those you work with at the human level, you raise their Relatedness reward. Thereafter, even technical disagreements can be more easily resolved because they see you as "friend," not "foe." If you are generous in acknowledging good ideas from people, you raise their Status reward and you may then find yourself on the receiving end of many other valuable ideas and solutions. If you are the boss and go the extra mile to be fair to your people, you raise their Fairness reward and they become much more willing to work for you. Thus, skillful use of SCARF factors for the good for all creates a win-win situation for everyone and expands your influence.

Based on the insight above, here is a four-step plan for expanding the magnitude and reach of your influence.

1. Know that you already have influence. You already affect people. It is a simple matter of improving what you can already do.

2. Strengthen self-confidence. The more you are aware of and comfortable with your own strengths and weaknesses, the more confident you become and the more effectively you can influence people. Emotionally, people gravitate toward confidence, especially the type of self-confidence based on kindness and authenticity. The mindfulness practices in Chapters 2 and 3 and the self-awareness practices in Chapter 4 will help you with self-confidence.

3. Understand people and help them succeed. You can influence people more effectively if you understand them and try to help them achieve their goals in ways that also help you achieve yours. The empathy practices in Chapter 7 plus the compassion practices earlier in this chapter will help you with understanding and helping people. Your knowledge of the neuroscience of the social brain learned from the last section will also help you greatly.

4. Serve the greater good. While remembering to take care of your own self-interest, never forget to go beyond just serving self-interest. Act also for the good of the team, or the good of the company, or the good of the world. Inspire the same in others. When your goodness inspires others, you can influence them more effectively. The practices in Chapter 6 on motivation, and the compassion practices in this chapter, will help you develop your instinct for serving the greater good.

If there is a single word that summarizes all the practices that help expand your influence, I think that word is *goodness.* Goodness is very inspiring, and it inspires in a way that changes people. That is why, for example, Mahatma Gandhi was and still is so influential.

How Goodness Can Change a Man's Life in Ten Minutes

One touching example of how goodness can change a man's life was a personal story told to me by famous psychologist Dr. Paul Ekman.

Paul has had a very successful career as a psychologist. In fact, he was named by the American Psychological Association as one of 100 Most Eminent Psychologists of the 20th Century. Paul, however, suffered a very difficult childhood, so he grew up to be a very angry adult. He told me that every single week of his life, he experienced at least two episodes of explosive anger that led him to do or say something he would later regret.

In 2000, Paul was invited to speak at a Mind and Life Conference held in India in the presence of the Dalai Lama. Paul was reluctant to go because he did not take Buddhist monks seriously; he thought of them as a bunch of funny bald men in robes. His daughter, Eve, had to convince him to attend.

On the third day of the five-day conference, something very important happened to Paul. During a break between meetings, Eve and Paul went to sit with the Dalai Lama and spoke to him for about ten minutes. For the duration of that conversation, the Dalai Lama held Paul's hand. Those ten minutes had a profound impact on Paul. He said he experienced an abundance of "goodness" within his entire being. He was transformed. By the end of those ten minutes, he found his anger completely fading away. For many weeks after that, he did not experience any trace of anger at all, which for him, was a huge life change. Perhaps more importantly, it changed the direction of his life. Paul was planning to retire, but after those ten minutes of holding the Dalai Lama's hand, he rediscovered his deep aspiration to bring benefit to the world, which was the reason he entered psychology in the first place. After some slight prodding from the Dalai Lama, Paul canceled his retirement plans and has since been giving his experience and wisdom to scientific research that may help people improve emotional balance, compassion, and altruism.

Goodness is so powerful that even experiencing it for just ten minutes can change a man's life. It does not even matter that the experience may be entirely subjective. In Paul's case, for example, the Dalai Lama claimed he did not do anything special, suggesting that the goodness Paul experienced came more from what Paul himself brought to the situation, with the Dalai Lama being merely a facilitator. Either way, the lesson is unmistakable: if you want to influence people, there is no greater power than goodness.

(Confession: I am comfortable using the word *goodness* only because Paul uses the word himself. If the word *goodness* is good enough for Paul Ekman, it is good enough for me.)

"Okay, now try projecting influence without using the Jedi mind trick."

Communicating with Insight

Empathy is a necessary ingredient for effective communication, but empathy is not always enough. I have seen even empathetic people get themselves into very frustrating conversations. The missing element is insight, specifically insight into the often hidden elements of a conversation, such as the identity issues involved and what impact was caused versus what was intended.

In the next section, we look at a framework from Harvard for conducting difficult conversations that will help us develop the necessary insight.

Difficult Conversations

Difficult conversations are conversations that are hard to have. They are often important, but because they are hard, we would usually rather avoid them. Two classic examples of difficult conversations in the workplace are asking for a raise and giving a valued employee critical feedback. It does not always have to be so drastic, however. Sometimes, even something as minor as asking your neighbor to not bring out the trash on non-trash days can be a difficult conversation.

Conducting difficult conversations is a skill, an extremely useful one, indeed. According to the authors of *Difficult Conversations,* who make up part of the Harvard Negotiation Project, there are five steps to conducting a difficult conversation. Here is my brief of those steps:

1. Prepare by walking through the "three conversations."
2. Decide whether to raise the issue.
3. Start from the objective "third story."
4. Explore their story and yours.
5. Problem solve.[9]

Prepare by Walking Through the "Three Conversations"

A powerful first step in improving our ability to conduct difficult conversations is understanding their underlying structure. In every conversation, there are actually three conversations going on. They are the content conversation ("What happened?"), the feelings conversation ("What emotions are involved?"), and the identity conversation ("What does this say about me?"). The identity conversation almost always involves one of these three questions:

1. Am I competent?
2. Am I a good person?
3. Am I worthy of love?

This step involves understanding the structure of the three conversations and preparing for them. Sort out what happened as objectively as possible, understand how this is impacting you and the other party emotionally, and identify what is at stake for you, *about* you.

Decide Whether to Raise the Issue

What do you hope to accomplish by raising this issue? Is it a productive intention (for example, to solve a problem, to help somebody develop themselves) or is it a nonproductive intention (for example, just wanting to make someone feel bad)? Sometimes, the right thing to do is not to raise the issue at all. If you decide to raise the issue, try shifting into a mode that supports learning and problem solving.

Start from the Objective "Third Story"

The "Third Story" is the way things happened from the perspective of a disinterested third-party who is aware of the whole situation. For example, if Matthew and I are having an argument, each of us will have our own version of what led to this argument. The narrative from our co-worker,

John, who knows everything that happened but is totally uninvolved, is the third story.

The third story is the best one with which to start a difficult conversation. It is the most objective and the one with which you are most likely to form a common ground with the other party. Use this third story to invite the other party to join you as a partner in sorting out the situation together.

Explore Their Story and Yours

Listen to their story. Empathize. Share your story. Explore how you each perceive the same situation differently. Reframe the stories from one of blame and accusation to one of learning about how each contributes to the situation and the emotions involved.

Problem Solve

Invent solutions that meet each side's most important concerns and interests. Find ways to continue keeping communications open and taking care of each other's interests.

Insights and Exercise for Difficult Conversations

Happily, if you have been working hard on all the practices in *Search Inside Yourself*, you have already acquired most of the skills you need to conduct difficult conversations. The only thing you need is to acquire two key insights.

The first key insight is that impact is not the intention. For example, if we feel hurt by something somebody said, we may automatically assume that the person intended to hurt us. In other words, we assume that the impact is the intention. Usually, we judge ourselves by our intentions, but we judge others by the impact of their behavior because we do not really know their intentions, so we subconsciously infer their intentions based on the impact of their behavior. In many situations, however, the impact is not the intention. For example, when Henry's wife told him to stop and ask for directions, he felt belittled, but she honestly did not set out intending to belittle his sense of manhood; she merely intended to arrive at the party on time. Her impact was not her intention. Let her know the impact on you, Henry, but do not start a fight with her. She meant no harm. (True story, though the name has been changed to protect every husband in the world, except Henry.)

The second key insight is that beyond the content and emotions in every difficult conversation, there are, more importantly, issues of identity. Very often the identity issues are the most hidden and left unsaid, but they are usually the most dominant. For example, if my manager wants to talk to me about the slow progress of my project, the thing that will bother me most is not the content of that conversation, or my feelings of anxiety, but my self-doubt concerning my own competence. In other words, the thing that will most bother me is the identity issue of "Am I competent?" Recognizing this, a skillful communicator makes sure she is aware of the identity issues and addresses them when appropriate. For example, being the skillful communicator that she is, my manager may begin the conversation by assuring me that she has full confidence in my competence; the thing she really wants to understand is what additional resources I may need. By addressing my identity issue skillfully right at the beginning, the entire quality of the conversation changes.

These two key insights are most relevant for Step 1 of the difficult conversation framework: prepare by walking through the "three conversations." If you have been doing your Search Inside Yourself practices, you should already be quite comfortable with all the other steps. Hence, we only need to pay extra attention to Step 1.

The best way to prepare for a difficult conversation is to talk to other people. That is because having people to talk to gives you the opportunity to verbalize and rehearse key parts of the difficult conversation beforehand. The best people to talk to are those you can trust, such as a best friend, a mentor, or a trusted peer at work. If you prefer to work alone, you may do it as a writing exercise instead.

PREPARING FOR A DIFFICULT CONVERSATION

You may do this as either a writing exercise or a speaking exercise. If you do this as a speaking exercise, you may speak to a friend.

Instructions

1. Think of a difficult conversation you had in the past, or one that you intend to have in the near future, or one that you should have had but did not.
2. Either in writing or spoken in a monologue, describe the "three conversations" from your own point of view. The three conversations are: the content conversation ("What happened?"), the feelings conversation ("What emotions are involved?"), and the identity conversation ("What does this say about me?"). The identity conversation almost always involves one of these three questions:
   - Am I competent?
   - Am I a good person?
   - Am I worthy of love?
3. Now, pretend that you are the other person and describe the three conversations from his or her point of view to the best of your abilities.

If you did this as a speaking exercise with a friend, discuss what it felt like for you in a free-flow conversation.

"How about now? Is now a good time to do the Difficult Conversations exercise?"

Mindful E-Mailing

The good news about modern communications is we do not have to do it face-to-face—we can use e-mail. The bad news is we do not do it face-to-face—we use e-mail. Yes, the good news is that we can, and the bad news is that we do.

The biggest problem with e-mail is that the emotional context is often miscommunicated, sometimes with disastrous results. When we talk to another person face-to-face, most of the emotions we communicate with each other are done nonverbally, usually with our facial expressions, tone of voice, postures, and gestures. In other words, our brains get to send and receive enough nonverbal information to do an "emotional tango" (see Chapter 7) that lets us communicate to each other what we are feeling. Most of that communication happens unconsciously. When we communicate via e-mail, however, we lose that entire mechanism for communicating feelings. When brains can't dance together, feelings don't get to tether.

But wait, it gets worse. When the brain receives insufficient data about others' feelings, it just makes stuff up. The brain makes assumptions about the emotional context of the message and then fabricates the missing information accordingly. It does not just fabricate information, however. It also automatically believes those fabrications to be true. Worse still, those fabrications usually have a strong negative bias—we usually assume people to have more negative intentions than they actually do.

For example, when Google's executive chairman, Eric Schmidt, saw me in the hallway, he wagged his finger at me mischievously and said with a big smile, "You, troublemaker." Since my brain was able to receive all the nonverbal cues, I knew he was just teasing me, so I never worried that he was going to fire me. However, if I had received those same words from him via e-mail, I might already be packing my stuff at the office and waiting for the lady at HR to come, err . . . discuss an important matter with me. That is true even if Eric had used a smiley in his e-mail.

That is why there is so much miscommunication over e-mail. We frequently get offended or frightened by e-mails that were never intended to offend or frighten. If we are emotionally unskillful, then we react with offense or fear, and then all hell breaks loose. I am not sure if the devil invented e-mail, but I am sure it made his job easier.

This is the key insight necessary for effective e-mail communications: because e-mails seldom contain sufficient information for the brain to recognize the emotional context of the sender, the brain fabricates the missing information, often with a negative bias, and then unconsciously assumes its own fabrication to be the truth.

Fortunately, mindfulness can help vastly improve the quality of your e-mail communications. The original Pali word that gets translated into "mindfulness" is *sati.* Sati also has an alternative translation: recollection (or reflection). That means that mindfulness is not just a mind of calmness, but it also has a strong quality of remembering and reflecting on insights.

When we engage in mindful e-mailing, that recollecting quality of mindfulness is the main one we rely on. The first thing we recollect is that there is a human being on the other end, a human being just like me. The second thing we recollect is this insight that people who receive e-mails unconsciously fabricate missing information about the emotional context of the sender, so we apply the appropriate care and caution.

Given that, here is the practice for mindful e-mailing.

PRACTICE OF MINDFUL E-MAILING

1. Begin by taking one conscious breath. If this is a particularly sensitive situation, calm your mind with a few minutes of Mindfulness Meditation (see Chapter 2) or Walking Meditation (see Chapter 3).
2. Mindfully reflect that on the receiving end, there are one or more human beings. Human beings just like me. If this is a particularly difficult situation, it may be useful to visualize the receiver or receivers in your mind and to engage in a few minutes of the Just Like Me / Loving Kindness exercise (see Chapter 7).
3. Write your e-mail.
4. Before sending, mindfully reflect on the insight that if the emotional context of your message is unclear, the receiver's brain will just make something up that is likely more negative than you intended. Put yourself in the receiver's shoes, pretend you know nothing about the sender's (your) emotional context, pretend also that you have a negative bias, and read your e-mail. Revise your e-mail if necessary.
5. Take one conscious breath before pressing Send. If this is a particularly delicate situation—for example if you are writing an angry e-mail to your boss or your subordinate—take three slow, conscious breaths before pressing Send. Feel free to change your mind about pressing Send.

Meng's Magic Mushroom Mantra

Let us close this chapter with a mantra that I created for myself. It summarizes many of my social skills practices. The mantra is:

Love them. Understand them. Forgive them. Grow with them.

Whenever I find myself in a difficult situation involving other people, I silently repeat the mantra to myself. It usually works. It works especially well with children and bosses.

My friend Rigel suggested that my mantra may also apply to magic mushrooms (very funny, Rigel), hence the name of the mantra.

CHAPTER NINE

Three Easy Steps to World Peace

The Story Behind Search Inside Yourself

To reach peace, teach peace.

—Pope John Paul II

Search Inside Yourself started with a simple dream, and that dream is world peace.

Like many others wiser than me, I believe world peace can and must be created from the inside out. If we can find a way for everybody to develop peace and happiness within themselves, their inner peace and happiness will naturally manifest into compassion. And if we can create a world where most people are happy, at peace, and compassionate, we can create the foundation for world peace.

Fortunately, a methodology for doing that already exists and has already been practiced by various peoples for thousands of years. It is the art of using contemplative practices to develop the mind. Most of us know it as meditation.

Meditation, at its simplest, is the training of attention. With enough meditative training, one's attention can become unwaveringly calm and focused. With that enhanced quality of attention, one's mind can easily, and for extended periods, become highly relaxed and alert at the same time. With that combination of relaxation and alertness, three wonderful qualities of mind naturally emerge: calmness, clarity, and happiness. Here's an analogy: Think of the mind as a snow globe that is shaken constantly. When you stop shaking the snow globe, the white "snow" particles within it eventually settle, and the fluid in the snow globe becomes calm and clear at the same time. Similarly, the mind is normally in a constant state of agitation. With deep mental relaxation and alertness, the mind settles into calmness and clarity. In this mind, the third quality, inner happiness, naturally emerges.

Inner happiness is contagious. When a person allows her inner glow of happiness to emerge, people around her tend to respond to her more positively. The meditator then finds her social interactions becoming increasingly positive, and because we are social creatures, positive social interactions create more happiness within her. A happy virtuous cycle of inner and social happiness thus establishes. As this cycle becomes stronger, the meditator finds herself becoming increasingly kinder and more compassionate.

We can train and develop the mind to create inner peace, happiness, and compassion. The best part of this training is that we do not even have to force ourselves to have those qualities; they are all naturally already within each of us, and all we need to do is create the conditions for them to emerge, grow, and flourish. We create those conditions through meditation. With meditation, we allow ourselves to become much happier and much more compassionate, and if enough of us do that, we create the foundation for world peace.

Hence, in a serious way that is almost comical, the key active ingredient in the formula for world peace may be something as simple as meditation.

It's such a simple solution to such an intractable problem, it is almost absurd. Except it may actually work.

This insight led me to an epiphany. I have found my life's goal. My life's goal is to make the benefits of meditation accessible to humanity. Note that I am not trying to bring meditation to the world. I am not even trying to bring its benefits to the world. All I intend to do is to make its benefits accessible. That is all. All I am doing is opening the door to the treasure room and telling people, "Here, all this treasure you see, feel free to take as much of it as you want, or not." I am merely a door opener. I am confident that the transformative power of contemplative practices is so compelling, anybody who understands it will find it irresistible. It is kind of like offering the secrets of health (for example, hygiene, nutrition, exercise, and sleep) to unhealthy people. Once people understand and begin to experience the benefits of health, there is no going back; it is just too compelling.

But, how? How does one make the benefits of meditation accessible to humanity? The answer to that question is something I half jokingly call the Three Easy Steps to World Peace.

1. Start with me.

2. Make meditation a field of science.

3. Align meditation with real life.

Start with Me

The first step is the most obvious, and it's attributed to Mahatma Gandhi: I need to become the change that I want to see in the world. To this end, I came up with an almost measurable goal for myself—that before the end of my lifetime, I want to create in myself the capacity to be kind to everyone, all the time. I want to be the Kindness Channel: all kindness, all day.

Make Meditation a Field of Science

To become widely accessible, meditation needs to become a field of science the same way medicine became a field of science. Like meditation, medicine had been practiced for countless generations, but ever since medicine became a field of science starting in the nineteenth century (beginning, perhaps, with Pasteur's research into microorganisms), everything about medicine has changed. I think the most important change was access. When medicine became scientific, it became greatly demystified; new tools, equipment, and methodologies became available; and training and certification of service providers greatly improved. In other words, a lot more people gained access to good medicine. I want to see the same thing happen to meditation.

Back in 2006, I wrote an e-mail (more of a mini manifesto) to my meditating friends, explaining that meditation needs to become scientific and inviting all to initiate an effort to make meditation training "data driven." The response I got back was completely underwhelming. People generally liked the idea, but nobody was particularly excited by it.

I finally found one person excited by it. My friend Tenzin Tethong forwarded my e-mail to Dr. B. Alan Wallace. Alan replied to me immediately and told me excitedly that he had been working on a similar effort for the past six years. Why? Because the Dalai Lama told him to! I was amazed. None of my meditating friends (many of them men and women of science) were excited by the marriage of meditation and science, but the Dalai Lama was. It was then that I knew I was on the right track. Surely His Holiness and I cannot both be wrong at the same time.

Alan and I became good friends very quickly. After a while, through learning more about Alan's work and related research by other scientists, I concluded that given the Dalai Lama's enthusiastic support, this effort was going to move forward with or without me. I did a few other things on this front, including becoming a founding patron of Stanford University's

Center for Compassion and Altruism Research and Education (CCARE) with the Dalai Lama and my friends Jim Doty and Wayne Wu. Ultimately, though, I decided this movement was in good hands and that I would instead focus my personal energy on Step 3.

Align Meditation with Real Life

For the benefits of meditation to become widely accessible to humanity, it cannot just be the domain of bald people in funny robes living in mountains, or small groups of New Age folks in San Francisco. Meditation needs to become "real." It needs to align with the lives and interests of real people, the average Joes of the world. This, I suspect, is the most important of the three steps, and the one where I can make the most impact. But how?

The historical precedence for this is exercise. In 1927, a group of scientists started the Harvard Fatigue Laboratory (HFL) to study the physiology of fatigue. Their pioneering work created the field of exercise physiology. One of their most important findings was that a fit person becomes physiologically different from an unfit person. With the benefit of hindsight, it is easy to see that their work has changed the world.

Today, thanks to the contribution of those pioneers and others, exercise has acquired at least four important features:

1. Everybody knows that "Exercise is good for me." There is no more debate. While it is true that not everybody takes the trouble to work out, even those who don't work out know that they should and that it would be good for them.

2. Anyone who wants to exercise can learn how to do it. The information is widely available, trainers are readily accessible if you want one, and many people have friends who work out who can show them how to exercise.

3. Companies understand that healthy and physically fit workers are good for business. Many companies even have gyms or provide subsidies for gym memberships.

4. Exercise is taken for granted. Exercise is so taken for granted today that when you tell your friends you are going to the gym to work out, nobody looks at you funny and thinks you are some New Age crank from San Francisco. In fact, it is now the reverse. If you, for example, argue that a pious American should never exercise, people look at you funny.

In other words, exercise has now perfectly aligned with the modern lives of real people. It has become fully accessible to all, and humanity benefits from it. I aspire to do the same with meditation. I want to create a world where meditation is widely treated like exercise for the mind, possessing all four features of exercise discussed above:

1. Everybody knows that "Meditation is good for me."

2. Anyone who wants to meditate can learn how to do it.

3. Companies understand that meditation is good for business, and some even incentivize it.

4. Meditation is taken for granted. Everybody thinks, "Of course you should meditate, duh."

Once again, we return to the same question: how? How do I create a world where meditation is taken for granted like exercise is? After a few months of working on the problem, I found the answer, almost by accident.

The answer came when I read Daniel Goleman's *Emotional Intelligence.* My friend Dr. Larry Brilliant, who was then the executive director of Google's philanthropic arm, had been a close friend of Daniel Goleman for a very long time. Dan was visiting Google to speak. Larry took the opportunity to hang out with him and invited me to come along. Out of courtesy to Dan, I decided to read *Emotional Intelligence* before meeting him. Reading that book gave me another epiphany. I had found my vehicle for aligning meditation with real life, and that vehicle is emotional intelligence (EI, sometimes known as EQ) .

You see, everybody already has a rough idea of what emotional intelligence is. More importantly, everybody knows that emotional intelligence is very useful for us. Even without fully understanding EI, many people know or suspect that EI will help them fulfill their worldly goals in life, such as becoming more effective at work, getting promotions, earning more money, working more effectively with other people, being admired, having fulfilling relationships, and so on. In other words, EI aligns perfectly with the needs and desires of modern people.

EI has two more important features. First, beyond helping you succeed, the greatest side effect of EI is increased inner happiness, empathy, and compassion for people, precisely what we need for world peace. Second, a very good way (and I suspect the only way) to truly develop EI is with contemplative practices starting with Mindfulness Meditation.

Eureka! I found it!

The way to create the conditions for world peace is to create a mindfulness-based emotional intelligence curriculum, perfect it within Google, and then give it away as one of Google's gifts to the world. The alignment is perfect. Everybody already wants EI, businesses already want EI, and we can help them achieve it. They can then become more effective at achieving their own goals *and* at the same time create the foundations for world peace.

When I finally met Dan, I could hardly contain myself. I was passionately explaining my world peace plan to him, almost banging on the table. I said, "This is world peace we're talking about, Danny, world peace!" Dan was visibly a little uncomfortable. There he was, coming to Google and meeting a bunch of Larry's friends and co-workers for the first time, and then there's this crazy young guy with a funny job title wanting to create world peace. The scene was a bit comical. Yes, the road to changing the world is often paved with moments of comic absurdity.

Dan and I subsequently became friends. Through Dan's and Larry's connections, I got to know two more amazing people, Mirabai Bush and Norman Fischer. Mirabai was the executive director of the Center for Contemplative Mind in Society, a very compassionate woman who was a very close friend of both Dan and Larry and who, like Larry, gave her adult life to the service of humanity. Norman is one of the most famous Zen masters in America today. I was especially impressed by Norman. He is very wise, intelligent, and knowledgeable; deeply spiritual yet grounded in worldly reality; and very good at applying deep practices to daily life. With Dan, Mirabai, and Norman, I now had people with curriculum expertise. All I needed was to convince somebody in Google to sponsor this course, and Google University (the internal employee education program now called GoogleEDU) eventually did.

Under the sponsorship of Google University, Mirabai, Norman, and I worked to create a curriculum for a mindfulness-based EI course, while Dan became our advisor, offering us the gift of his expertise and wisdom. While sitting in a room with Mirabai and Norman, I realized all three of us were radiant beings. Mirabai radiated compassion, Norman radiated wisdom, and I radiated ambient body heat.

The curriculum team eventually expanded to include three more highly talented individuals with a diversity of talents. Marc Lesser is the founder and former CEO of Brush Dance Publishing and the author of two business books, and he brought real-life business expertise and content. Philippe Goldin is a neuroscience researcher at Stanford University, and he brought scientific breadth and depth. Yvonne Ginsberg is a practicing therapist who taught at Yale University, and she deepened the personal dimension of the curriculum. All three are also highly respected meditation teachers in their own rights. Now we have real mojo.

In parallel with curriculum development, I formed an extremely diverse all-volunteer team to implement the course. The team consisted of Joel Finkelstein, a massage therapist; David Lapedis, a recruiter; Dr. Hongjun Zhu, an engineer; Rachel Kay, a learning specialist; and me, the jolly good fellow of Google. Dr. Peter Allen, then the director of Google

University, was the patron saint of the project and an active participant. Members of the team were promised absolutely nothing in return for their thankless, unpaid hard work—except the opportunity to create world peace. Surprisingly, they all wanted in. It's amazing what people will do for world peace.

The name of the course is Search Inside Yourself (SIY). Joel suggested it. Everybody laughed when he did. I didn't really like the name at first, but my philosophy is if everybody laughs, it must be the right thing to do. So I agreed to it.

Search Inside Yourself has been taught in Google since 2007, benefiting hundreds of people and sometimes changing their lives. It has become effective enough that we are now ready to "open source" it and make it accessible outside Google. This book is part of that effort.

And the rest, as they say, is the future.

EPILOGUE

Save the World in Your Free Time

Insert funny quote here in your free time.

I once took a long walk with Zen master Roshi Joan Halifax, a dear friend who is like a sister to me. I sometimes joke about her being my "little sister" because she is only thirty years older than me. During our walk, we talked about our lives, the spiritual practice of non-doing and about our aspirations toward service to the world ("saving the world," we joked). We also joked about the contradiction in aspiring to both be lazy, cushion-sitting meditators and tireless bodhisattvas (world saviors) at the same time.

What I remember most about the conversation was how inspired I was by Roshi's being. Roshi is one of the most compassionate souls I have ever had the honor to meet. You can tell just by looking at her eyes—she has the most gentle, compassionate eyes of anybody I know. Among the many amazing things she has quietly done in her life, she has spent many decades serving and comforting the dying. She is also a Zen abbot and a board member of the Mind and Life Institute, which continues to benefit many people.

Roshi is always busy giving of herself to benefit other people, yet you feel that she is just having fun doing what comes most naturally to her. I reflected on Roshi's being, and it occurred to me that hers is a common theme among all the inspiring, enlightened individuals with whom I have had the honor of spending time: Sadhguru Jaggi Vasudev, a yoga master whose organization also holds the world record for the highest number of trees planted in a single day; A. T. Ariyaratne ("Dr. Ari"), a humble English teacher who felt inspired to go around helping people and ended up founding the largest NGO in Sri Lanka; Matthieu Ricard, who in addition to being the happiest man in the world also runs a humanitarian organization benefiting many people without getting any pay; and of course, the Dalai Lama.

All these bodhisattvas think of their tireless work for humanity as little more than having fun by doing whatever comes most naturally to them. They sometimes joke about themselves as being "lazy," even though they are often busier than many overstressed business executives I know.

The Dalai Lama, for example, despite his busy schedule, said, "I don't do anything." They are also all very joyful. Sadhguru said my job title of jolly good fellow should be his too.

My epiphany is that "saving the world" is so hard and takes so much effort that if you strive hard to "save the world," it is not likely to be sustainable. Instead, it is more skillful to focus on developing inner peace, compassion, and aspiration. When inner peace, compassion, and aspiration are all strong, compassionate action comes naturally and organically, and hence, it is sustainable.

The great Zen master Thich Nhat Hanh, another one of those bodhisattvas tirelessly serving the world, and who also calls himself a "lazy monk," says it beautifully: "With all this socially engaged work, first you must learn what the Buddha learned, to still the mind. Then you don't take action; action takes you."

You don't take action, action takes you.

Inspired, I wrote this poem:

THE LAZY BODHISATTVA

With deep inner peace,
And great compassion,
Aspire daily to save the world.
But do not strive to achieve it.
Just do whatever comes naturally.
Because when aspiration is strong
And compassion blossoms,
Whatever comes most naturally,
Is also the right thing to do.
Thus you,
The wise compassionate being,
Save the world while having fun.

My friend, may you be lazy, and may you save the world.

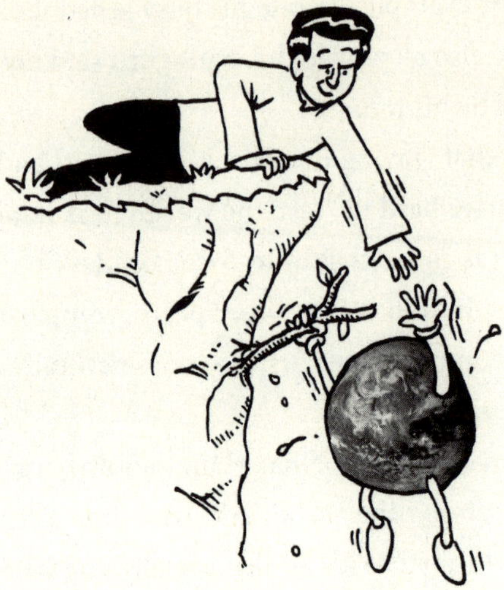

Acknowledgments

If I have seen a little further it is by standing on the shoulders of Giants.

—Isaac Newton

Hey, there is some guy standing on our shoulders.

—Giants

This book is about applying wisdom in the real world, but none of that wisdom actually came from me. The wisdom is already everywhere, practiced, taught, and embodied by countless generations of wise men and women, many of whom live among us. I see great people. Walking around like regular people. They don't even know they are great.

No, I did not generate wisdom. All I did was translate it into terms that even I can understand. I am merely a translator for the wise ones. In a way, they are the real authors of this book and I am just the guy typing on the keyboard.

First and foremost, I want to give thanks to my main drinking source of that wisdom. He is a man so dear to me and whose teachings I have become so intimate with that, in my heart, I endearingly refer to him as "the Old Man." Others know him as the Buddha. I am also deeply grateful to those who have passed down his teachings and especially those who passed those teachings directly to me. Among them are the late Godwin Samararatne (my first meditation teacher); the Venerables

Sangye Khadro, Bhikkhu Bodhi, S. Dhammika, and Matthieu Ricard; the Very Venerable Yongey Mingyur Rinpoche; Zen Masters Thich Nhat Hanh, Norman Fischer, Shinzen Young, and Joan Halifax; and lay teachers Jon Kabat-Zinn, Shaila Catherine, and Alan Wallace. I am grateful to His Holiness the Dalai Lama for exemplifying great wisdom, compassion, and humor in the modern world, and also for giving me a hug for my fortieth birthday. He made turning forty almost bearable for me. I am thankful to all of them and many others for deepening my mind.

I am thankful to many who showed me the same wisdom and compassion in the context of faith traditions. I was deeply touched reading the Sermon on the Mount and learning about the life of Jesus Christ. I am thankful to a beautiful woman I met in college, Cindy, for introducing Him to me. I later managed to con, I mean, convince her to marry me. Many other dear friends reinforced my attraction to Jesus. One of them is a Benedictine monk, Brother David Steindl-Rast, who impressed me with his deep serenity and gentle humor. Another is Dr. Stuart Lord, a Baptist minister who also manages to be a Buddhist meditator running a major Buddhist university. Other dear friends like Norman Fischer showed me that you can be a practicing Jew and Buddhist (in his case, a classically-trained Buddhist Zen master) at the same time. I am thankful to all of them and many others for opening my mind.

There is a story I need to tell: Once upon a time, there were three highly talented young men who wanted to serve the world and who became close friends with each other. Their names were Danny, Richie, and Jon. When they grew up, they each became world famous in their own unique ways, but the success of each one beautifully complemented the success of the other two. Danny is Daniel Goleman. He became a highly successful author who popularized emotional intelligence. Richie is Richard J. Davidson. He became a highly respected scientist who, among numerous achievements, pioneered much of the science behind contemplative practices. Jon is Jon Kabat-Zinn. He became the first person to bring mindfulness into mainstream medicine and, in the process, brought mindfulness into mainstream modern culture. My work would have been impossible without any one of them. If Danny hadn't popularized emotional intelligence, or Richie hadn't pioneered the neuroscience, or Jon hadn't introduced mindfulness into the mainstream, Search Inside Yourself would not be successful. I stand on the shoulders of these giants. I'm happy for them that I'm not too fat, at least not yet.

I am grateful to the Search Inside Yourself team for the work that directly inspired this book. I want to thank Daniel Goleman again, whose active support made Search Inside Yourself possible. I want to thank the Search Inside Yourself instructors for not only creating the curriculum but also being my teachers. They are Norman Fischer, Mirabai Bush, Marc Lesser, Yvonne Ginsberg, and Philippe Goldin, every one of whom taught me something valuable. I thank the core Search Inside Yourself team for doing the actual work of making it happen: Hongjun Zhu, Joel Finkelstein, David Lapedis, Rachel Kay, Albert Hwang, Monika Broecker, Jenny Lykken, Terry Okamoto, and Sara McCleskey, and many others who have volunteered their help in some way. Albert and Jenny deserve special mention for creating some parts of the curriculum and helping us teach some classes even though they were not formally on the instructors team; they are both talented far beyond their years. I would also like to thank the early bosses of GoogleEDU (known back then as Google University) for approving Search Inside Yourself, especially to Peter Allen for being our first "patron saint" as the then director of Google University and, his manager, Paul Russell for giving us the final approval and his subsequent unrelenting support. Paul modestly jokes that his biggest contribution to Search Inside Yourself is "not saying no." I also want to thank other managers at Google for their vital support at various times: Jun Liu, Erica Fox, Stephan Thoma, Evan Wittenberg, and Karen May. I want to especially thank Karen not just for being the best manager I have ever had but also for being an example of what a highly empathetic manager is like. Karen is the most empathetic person I have ever worked with; I call her the Queen of Empathy. She is one of those rare senior managers who is widely beloved by her people.

I am thankful to all the highly talented people who, in their moments of weakness, agreed to work with me on this book. Chief among them is Colin Goh, my friend, advisor, and illustrator. Colin is an award-winning cartoonist and filmmaker with a law degree—what's not to love about that? Christina Marini was my talented and tireless research assistant—if any of you ever need to employ anybody, you'll be lucky to have her. Jill Stracko advised me on various aspects of writing and gave me her time to edit various iterations of early drafts. Jill used to head the White House writing staff, so I feel really honored to be on the receiving end of her generosity and wisdom. My agent, Stephanie Tade, was a rare find. When I advertised for an agent, I set an unreasonably high bar for who I wanted to work with. Among many requirements, I wanted somebody with a solid meditation practice who is driven primarily by compassion, is highly successful at what she does, and yet is open to doing things in entirely unconventional ways. I didn't expect her to even exist, but I found her within two weeks. Thanks to Jim Gimian and Bob Stahl for helping me find her. I have learned a lot from my editor, Gideon Weil, and have really enjoyed working with him and everyone else at HarperOne, including the publisher, Mark Tauber. I want to thank Philippe Goldin and Thomas Lewis for giving me valuable scientific advice. Last but not least, I am thankful to friends who took the time to read through my early drafts in their entirety and have given me many useful suggestions, including HueAnh Nguyen, Rich Hua, Olivia Fox, Audrey Tan, Tom Oliver, Kian-Jin Jek, Tomithy Too, and Kathrin O'Sullivan.

I am deeply thankful to my parents for keeping me nourished and sheltered (no small feat during my early Asian childhood) and for keeping me out of trouble for all my formative years. I am also deeply thankful to my lovely wife, Cindy, for (still) keeping me. Last but not least, I am grateful to my daughter, Angel, for being the greatest love of my life and for loving me back.

For those of you whom I owe a lot to, let me repay you partially with this poem, mostly because it costs me nothing:

Let's go, vamanos.

Beyond the limited mind.

Everybody let's go.

Welcome to enlightenment!

(In original Sanskrit: Gate, gate. Paragate. Parasamgate. Bodhi svaha*!)*

Notes

Introduction:
Searching Inside Yourself

1. The full story on the adventures of Matthieu Ricard in the lab is available in the first chapter of the book *Destructive Emotions: How Can We Overcome Them?: A Scientific Dialogue with the Dalai Lama,* by Daniel Goleman (New York: Random House, 2004). It is also available as a story titled "The Lama in the Lab" in the March 2003 issue of *Shambhala Sun.* Highly recommended read.

2. Richard Davidson and William Irwin, "The Functional Neuroanatomy of Emotion and Affective Style," *Trends in Cognitive Sciences* 3, no. 1 (1999): 11–21. If you would like to learn more about the scientific research on that topic, the references in this more recent paper are also very useful: Richard Davidson, Alexander Shackman, and Jeffrey Maxwell, "Asymmetries in Face and Brain Related to Emotion," *Trends in Cognitive Sciences* 8, no. 9 (2004): 389–391.

Chapter One:
Even an Engineer Can Thrive on Emotional Intelligence

1. Peter Salovey and John D. Mayer, "Emotional Intelligence," *Imagination, Cognition, and Personality* 9, no. 3 (1990): 185–211.

2. This connection was first suggested to me by a short YouTube video titled "Scrooge and his Emotional Intelligence," http://siybook.com/v/scrooge.

3. Daniel Goleman, *Working with Emotional Intelligence* (New York: Bantam, 1998). The said studies are described in Chapter 3 and Appendix 2.

4. Martin E. Seligman, *Learned Optimism: How to Change Your Mind and Your Life* (New York: Vintage Books, 1990).

5. Daniel Goleman, "Social Intelligence: The New Science of Human Relationships" (lecture, Authors@Google, Mountain View, CA, August 3, 2007), http://siybook.com/v/gtalk_dgoleman.

6. Goleman, *Working with Emotional Intelligence.* The data analysis is described in Chapter 8 and Appendix 2.

7. Wallace Bachman, "Nice Guys Finish First: A SYMLOG Analysis of U.S. Naval Commands," in *The SYMLOG Practitioner,* ed. Polley, Hare, and Stone (New York: Praeger, 1988): 133–153.

8. Matthieu Ricard, *Happiness: A Guide to Developing Life's Most Important Skill* (New York: Little, Brown and Company, 2003).

9. Katherine Woollett, Hugo J. Spiers, and Eleanor A. Maguire, "Talent in the Taxi: A Model System for Exploring Expertise," *Philosophical Transactions of the Royal Society 8* 364, no. 1522 (2009): 1407–1416. There is also a BBC News article, available at: http://siybook.com/a/taxibrain.

10. Unpublished data. Philippe Goldin, Ph.D. "Cognitive Reappraisal of Emotion after Cognitive-Behavioral Therapy for Social Anxiety Disorder." Presented at the annual conference of the Association for Behavioral and Cognitive Therapies, Orlando, Fl, November 2008.

11. R. Christopher deCharms, et al., "Control Over Brain Activation and Pain Learned by Using Real-Time Functional MRI," *Proceedings of the National Academy of Sciences of the United States of America* 102, no. 51 (2005): 18626–18631. Also see: R. Christopher deCharms, "Reading and Controlling Human Brain Activation Using Real-Time Functional Magnetic Resonance Imaging," *Trends in Cognitive Sciences* 11, no. 11 (2007): 473–481.

12. Jon Kabat-Zinn, *Wherever You Go, There You Are: Mindfulness Meditation in Everyday Life* (New York: Hyperion, 1994).

13. Thich Nhat Hanh, *The Miracle of Mindfulness: An Introduction to the Practice of Meditation* (Boston: Beacon Press, 1999).

14. J. A. Brefczynski-Lewis, et al., "Neural Correlates of Attentional Expertise in Long-Term Meditation Practitioners," *Proceedings of the National Academy of Sciences of the United States of America* 104, no. 27 (2007): 11483–11488.

15. Matthew Lieberman, et al., "Putting Feelings into Words: Affect Labeling Disrupts Amygdala Activity in Response to Affective Stimuli," *Psychological Science* 18, no. 5 (2007): 421–428.

16. J. D. Creswell, et al., "Neural Correlates of Dispositional Mindfulness during Affect Labeling," *Psychosomatic Medicine* 69, no. 6 (2007): 560–565.

17. Laura Delizonna and Ted Anstedt, "Enhancing Emotional Intelligence" (unpublished manuscript, 2011). Also relevant is the famous James-Lange theory (by William James and Carl Lange) suggesting that changes in bodily responses are a necessary condition for emotional experience to arise.

18. Malcolm Gladwell, *Blink: The Power of Thinking Without Thinking* (New York: Little, Brown and Company, 2005).

19. Daniel Goleman, "Social Intelligence: The New Science of Human Relationships" (lecture, Authors@Google, Mountain View, CA, August 3, 2007), http://siybook.com/v/gtalk_dgoleman.

Chapter Two: Breathing as if Your Life Depends on It

1. Brefczynski-Lewis, "Neural Correlates of Attentional Expertise."

2. Actually, magic is at Platform 9¾ at King's Cross station, but I wasn't supposed to tell.

3. William James, *The Principles of Psychology*, vol. 1 (New York: MacMillan, 1890).

4. HH the Dalai Lama, *The Universe in a Single Atom: The Convergence of Science and Spirituality* (New York: Three Rivers Press, 2006).

5. Richard Davidson, et al., "Alterations in Brain and Immune Function Produced by Mindfulness Meditation," *Psychosomatic Medicine* 65, no. 4 (2003): 564–570.

6. Heleen Slagter, et al., "Mental Training Affects Distribution of Limited Brain Resources," *PloS Biology* 5, no. 6 (2007): e138.

7. Antoine Lutz, et al., "Long-Term Meditators Self-Induce High-Amplitude Gamma Synchrony during Mental Practice," *Proceedings of the National*

Academy of Sciences of the United States of America 101, no. 46 (2004): 16369–16373.

8. Jon Kabat-Zinn, et al., "Influence of a Mindfulness Meditation-Based Stress Reduction Intervention on Rates of Skin Clearing in Patients with Moderate to Severe Psoriasis Undergoing Phototherapy (UVB) and Photochemotherapy (PUVA)," *Psychosomatic Medicine* 60, no. 5 (1998): 625–632.
9. Sara Lazar, et al., "Meditation Experience Is Associated with Increased Cortical Thickness," *Neuroreport* 16, no. 17 (2005): 1893–1897.

Chapter Three: Mindfulness Without Butt on Cushion

1. James, *The Principles of Psychology.*
2. Thich Nhat Hanh, *The Miracle of Mindfulness.*
3. Norman Fischer, *Taking Our Places: The Buddhist Path to Truly Growing Up* (San Francisco: HarperOne, 2004).
4. Thich Nhat Hanh, *Living Buddha, Living Christ* (New York: Riverhead, 1997).
5. Personal communication.

Chapter Four: All-Natural, Organic Self-Confidence

1. Goleman, *Working with Emotional Intelligence.*
2. Goleman, *Working with Emotional Intelligence.* See "Emotional Competence Framework" for the definition of *self-awareness.*
3. Cary Cherniss and Daniel Goleman, *The Emotionally Intelligent Workplace: How to Select for, Measure, and Improve Emotional Intelligence in Individuals, Groups, and Organizations* (Hoboken, NJ: Jossey-Bass, 2001).
4. Cherniss and Goleman, *The Emotionally Intelligent Workplace.*
5. Fischer, *Taking Our Places.*
6. Richard Boyatzis, *The Competent Manager: A Model for Effective Performance* (New York: Wiley, 1982).

7. Alexander Stajkovic and Fred Luthans, "Self-Efficacy and Work-Related Performance: A Meta-Analysis," *Psychological Bulletin* 124, no. 2 (1998): 240–261.

8. Daniel Goleman, *Emotional Intelligence: Why It Can Matter More Than IQ* (New York: Bantam, 1995).

9. Kabat-Zinn, *Wherever You Go, There You Are.*

10. S. P. Spera, E. D. Buhrfeind, and J. W. Pennebaker, "Expressive Writing and Coping with Job Loss," *Academy of Management Journal* 37, no. 3 (1994): 722–733.

11. "Know Thyself," *Very Short List* (March 2, 2009), http://siybook.com/a/knowthyself.

Chapter Five: Riding Your Emotions like a Horse

1. "Lekha Sutta," the Discourse on Inscriptions, *Anguttara Nikaya.*

2. *Xinxin Ming,* Inscriptions on Trust in Mind. Also known as the *Shinjinmei* in Japanese.

3. Jon Kabat-Zinn, *Full Catastrophe Living: Using the Wisdom of Your Body and Mind to Face Stress, Pain, and Illness* (New York: Delacorte Press, 1990).

4. Philippe Goldin, "The Neuroscience of Emotions" (lecture, Google Tech Talks, Mountain View, CA, September 16, 2008), http://siybook.com/v/gtalk_pgoldin.

5. Kevin Ochsner and James Gross, "The Cognitive Control of Emotion," *Trends in Cognitive Sciences* 9, no. 5 (2005): 242–249.

6. Yongey Mingyur Rinpoche, *The Joy of Living: Unlocking the Secret and Science of Happiness* (New York: Harmony, 2007).

Chapter Six: Making Profits, Rowing Across Oceans, and Changing the World

1. Tony Hsieh, *Delivering Happiness: A Path to Profits, Passion, and Purpose* (New York: Business Plus, 2010).

2. John Geirland, "Go with the Flow," *Wired* 4, no. 9 (1996).
3. Daniel Pink, *Drive: The Surprising Truth About What Motivates Us* (New York: Riverhead, 2009).
4. Daniel Pink, "The Surprising Science of Motivation" (lecture, TEDGlobal, July 2009), http://siybook.com/v/ted_dpink.
5. According to *BusinessWeek*'s 2009 Customer Service Champs report—ranked by reader surveys and J. D. Power research—Zappos was ranked seventh while Four Seasons was ranked twelfth.
6. Marc Lesser, *Less: Accomplishing More by Doing Less* (Novato, CA: New World Library, 2009).
7. Michael Jordan on the Nike commercial, "Failure."
8. Brent Schlender, "Gates without Microsoft," *Fortune Magazine* (June 20, 2008).
9. Seligman, *Learned Optimism.*
10. Barbara Fredrickson, *Positivity: Groundbreaking Research Reveals How to Embrace the Hidden Strength of Positive Emotions, Overcome Negativity, and Thrive* (New York: Crown, 2009).
11. "Great Waves," *101zenstories.com.*

Chapter Seven:
Empathy and the Monkey Business of Brain Tangos

1. G. Rizzolatti and M. Fabbri-Destro, "Mirror Neurons: From Discovery to Autism," *Experimental Brain Research* 200, no. 3–4 (2010): 223–237.
2. A very nice, readable quick guide by Christian Keysers on mirror neurons is available in *Current Biology* 19, no. 21(2009): R971–R973. Also available on the web at: http://siybook.com/a/keysers.
3. An excellent survey on these and other scientific studies relating to empathy is: Tania Singer, "Understanding Others: Brain Mechanisms of Theory of Mind and Empathy" in *Neuroeconomics: Decision Making and the Brain,* eds. P. W. Glimcher, et al. (Maryland Heights, MO: Academic Press, 2008): 251–268.

4. There is a collection of studies each addressing a different aspect of the relationship between emotional awareness, empathy, and the insula. [Craig 2004] and [Herbert 2007] suggest significant links between strong emotional awareness and awareness of inner-body feelings via activity in the insula, including perception of heartbeats, while [Singer 2008] describes many studies that link the insula to empathy. [Lutz 2008] suggests all these abilities are trainable with meditation. [Craig 2004]: A. D. Craig, "Human Feelings: Why Are Some More Aware Than Others?" *Trends in Cognitive Sciences* 8, no. 6 (2004): 239–41. [Herbert 2007]: B. M. Herbert, O. Pollatos, and R. Schandry, "Interoceptive Sensitivity and Emotion Processing: An EEG Study," *International Journal of Psychophysiology* 65, no. 3 (2007): 214–227. [Lutz 2008]: A. Lutz, "Regulation of the Neural Circuitry of Emotion by Compassion Meditation: Effects of Meditative Expertise," *PLoS One* 3, no. 3 (2008): e1897. [Singer 2008]: Singer, "Understanding Others."

5. R. W. Levenson and A. M. Ruef, "Empathy: A Physiological Substrate," *Journal of Personality and Social Psychology* 63, no. 2 (1992): 234–246. More information on this topic is also available in R. W. Levenson and A. M. Ruef, "Physiological Aspects of Emotional Knowledge and Rapport" in *Empathic Accuracy,* ed. W. Ickes (New York: Guilford Press, 1997).

6. Goleman, *Working with Emotional Intelligence.*

7. A. Serino, G. Giovagnoli, and E. Làdavas, "I Feel What You Feel If You Are Similar to Me," *PLoS One* 4, no. 3 (2009): e4930.

8. "Dvedhavitakka Sutta," the Discourse on Two Kinds of Thoughts, *Majjhima Nikaya,* skillful thoughts that lead to long-term happiness and unskillful thoughts that lead to the type of trouble mom warned you about. And you thought mom was just being hysterical.

9. K. E. Buchanan and A. Bardi, "Acts of Kindness and Acts of Novelty Affect Life Satisfaction," *Journal of Social Psychology* 150, no. 3 (2010): 235–237.

10. Patrick Lencioni, *The Five Dysfunctions of a Team: A Leadership Fable* (Hoboken, NJ: Jossey-Bass, 2002).

11. C. M. Mueller and C. S. Dweck, "Praise for Intelligence Can Undermine Children's Motivation and Performance," *Journal of Personality and Social Psychology* 75, no. 1 (1998): 33–52.

12. Carol S. Dweck, *Mindset: The New Psychology of Success* (New York: Random House, 2006).

13. Goleman, *Working with Emotional Intelligence,* 160.

Chapter Eight:
Being Effective and Loved at the Same Time

1. James Kouzes and Barry Posner, *Encouraging the Heart: A Leader's Guide to Rewarding and Recognizing Others* (Hoboken, NJ: Jossey-Bass, 2003).

2. Bill George, *True North: Discover Your Authentic Leadership* (Hoboken, NJ: Jossey-Bass, 2007).

3. Jim Collins, *Good to Great: Why Some Companies Make the Leap . . . and Others Don't* (New York: HarperBusiness, 2001).

4. Barbara Fredrickson, *Positivity,* www.positivityratio.com.

5. John Gottman, *Why Marriages Succeed or Fail . . . and How You Can Make Yours Last* (New York: Simon & Schuster, 1994).

6. All the studies relating to the SCARF model mentioned in this book, except for the fairness studies on chimpanzees, can be found in the Notes section of this very good book: David Rock, *Your Brain at Work: Strategies for Overcoming Distraction, Regaining Focus, and Working Smarter All Day Long* (New York: HarperBusiness, 2009).

7. Rock, *Your Brain at Work.*

8. K. Jensen, J. Call, and M. Tomasello, "Chimpanzees Are Rational Maximizers in an Ultimatum Game," *Science* 318, no. 5847 (2007): 107–109.

9. Douglas Stone, Bruce Patton, and Sheila Heen, *Difficult Conversations: How to Discuss What Matters Most* (New York: Penguin, 1999).

Recommended Reading and Resources

Books

What, you still have time to read? Lucky you. I hardly have time to read my own book, and I adore the author, he's funny. For you, my friend, here are some books that will help you learn more about the topics covered in *Search Inside Yourself.*

Actually, all the books I mentioned in the footnotes of *Search Inside Yourself* are great reads, but if you only have time to read a small subset of those books, the books listed below constitute the short list I most highly recommend.

If you have time for only one more book after *Search Inside Yourself,* read *Difficult Conversations.* It is a very useful book—small, thin, and readable. You can read it in its entirety on a long flight, yet it tells you everything you need to know about the optimal steps to conducting difficult conversations. Highly recommended.

> Douglas Stone, Bruce Patton, and Sheila Heen, *Difficult Conversations: How to Discuss What Matters Most* (New York: Penguin, 1999).

If you would like to learn more about emotional intelligence, there is no better introduction than Daniel Goleman's *Emotional Intelligence.* There is a reason that book sold millions of copies, and it was not just Dan's good looks. If you want to read more about emotional intelligence in the context of work, Dan's *Working with Emotional Intelligence* is your best bet.

> Daniel Goleman, *Emotional Intelligence: Why It Can Matter More Than IQ* (New York: Bantam, 1995).

> Daniel Goleman, *Working with Emotional Intelligence* (New York: Bantam, 1998).

There are three books I highly recommend on mindfulness and meditation; you can read any one or all three. The first is Thich Nhat Hanh's *The Miracle of Mindfulness.* Thich Nhat Hanh is a great master who, in my eyes, personifies near perfection in mindfulness practice. *The Miracle of Mindfulness* is my favorite among his many good books. Thich Nhat Hanh originally wrote it as a long letter to a friend, so it presents mindfulness in an informal, personal, and heartwarming way.

Another very good book on mindfulness is Jon Kabat-Zinn's *Wherever You Go, There You Are.* This guide to mindfulness is highly sensible, easy to read, and poetically beautiful, and it presents the essence of mindfulness at a significant depth. In person, Jon is ultra-intelligent and embodies an impressively deep quality of mindfulness and heartfulness. His book reflects both his personality and his great skill as a teacher.

The third great meditation book I'll recommend here is Mingyur Rinpoche's *The Joy of Living.* Mingyur is a gem. He is a great meditation prodigy who overcame his panic disorder with the power of his mind at the age of thirteen, and he was appointed as a teacher at the tender age of sixteen. *The Joy of Living* is a wonderful meditation book intertwined with Mingyur's lovely life story.

Thich Nhat Hanh, *The Miracle of Mindfulness: An Introduction to the Practice of Meditation* (Boston: Beacon Press, 1999).

Jon Kabat-Zinn, *Wherever You Go, There You Are: Mindfulness Meditation in Everyday Life* (New York: Hyperion, 1994).

Yongey Mingyur Rinpoche, *The Joy of Living: Unlocking the Secret and Science of Happiness* (New York: Harmony, 2007).

If you have time to read only one of the three books above, I suggest *The Miracle of Mindfulness* because it is short and sweet.

If you are interested in the science, philosophy, and practices surrounding the transformation of destructive emotions, read Daniel Goleman's *Destructive Emotions.* (I know, the previous sentence can be quite funny when read aloud.) Dan's book captures a fascinating dialogue that occurred in the Dalai Lama's living room among some of the greatest minds in the world on that subject. If you are interested in the application of neuroscience specifically in the workplace, there is no better book that David Rock's *Your Brain at Work.* It is easy to read and action packed with detailed scientific references for those of us who need to teach social skills classes to engineers. I highly recommend both books, especially if you are a card-carrying member of the geek club, like I am.

Daniel Goleman, *Destructive Emotions: How Can We Overcome Them?: A Scientific Dialogue with the Dalai Lama* (New York: Random House, 2004).

David Rock, *Your Brain at Work: Strategies for Overcoming Distraction, Regaining Focus, and Working Smarter All Day Long* (New York: HarperBusiness, 2009).

Last but not least, I tell all my friends that if they only read a single business book in their lifetime, the one to read is Jim Collins's *Good to Great.* It will teach you more about running a great business than any other book I know of.

Jim Collins, *Good to Great: Why Some Companies Make the Leap . . . and Others Don't* (New York: HarperBusiness, 2001).

Videos

You are the type who prefers to watch a video rather than read a book? I have resources even for you, my video-preferring friend.

There is a great series of talks relating to personal growth hosted at Google, mostly by yours truly. The list of talks is available at: http://www.siybook.com/resources.

The three great talks that are most relevant to us are the ones delivered by the three close friends whose work enabled us to create Search Inside Yourself. The three are Daniel Goleman, Jon Kabat-Zinn, and Richie Davidson. The videos are:

- Daniel Goleman on emotional intelligence: http://siybook.com/v/gtalk_dgoleman
- Jon Kabat-Zinn on mindfulness: http://siybook.com/v/gtalk_jkz
- Richie Davidson on contemplative neuroscience: http://siybook.com/v/gtalk_rdavidson

For those who enjoy brain science, three other great talks on the brain science that is relevant to Search Inside Yourself are:

- Philippe Goldin on the neuroscience of emotions: http://siybook.com/v/gtalk_pgoldin

- Thomas Lewis on the neuroscience of empathy: http://siybook.com/v/gtalk_tlewis
- David Rock on your brain at work: http://siybook.com/v/gtalk_drock

Of all the talks on meditation I've hosted at Google, my favorite is one by Zen master Shinzen Young:

- Shinzen Young on the science and practice of mindfulness meditation: http://siybook.com/v/gtalk_shinzen

Some of my favorite videos are of TED talks and can be found on www.ted.com. I'd like to highlight a few that people who enjoy *Search Inside Yourself* will find fascinating:

- Dan Pink on the surprising science of motivation: http://siybook.com/v/ted_dpink
- Jill Bolte Taylor on her "stroke of insight": http://siybook.com/v/ted_jbt
- V. S. Ramachandran on what brain damage can teach us about the mind: http://siybook.com/v/ted_vsr
- Daniel Kahneman on how our "experiencing selves" and "remembering selves" perceive happiness differently: http://siybook.com/v/ted_dkahneman
- Chade-Meng Tan on how compassion can be practiced in a corporate setting: http://siybook.com/v/ted_meng

The last TED talk on that list is my favorite—I don't know why.

Other Resources

For more resources, including those you can use to bring Search Inside Yourself to your own company, visit http://www.siybook.com.

Index